INTRODUCTION

GW00750178

There are those in the football world '
their are many who never were, those v
achieve whether through bad luck or t.._, ,

For myself I was a mixture of them all I was their and at least had a go injury and bad luck hampered the playing career, but of the pitch I achieved a lot more! My story is not Roy of the Rovers style as I was never the Sean Bean character in the film "When Saturday Comes", but I hope you find it entertaining.

Chapter 1
In The Blood

Football has been in the blood of my family for over a century now. We have had a mixed career!

The Latham family originate from the Liverpool and Wakefield areas, but in the 1870's a move down south happened. Most of my direct descendants arrived in a small house in Plumstead High Street. At that time the high street was mostly unnumbered, being comprised of a large number of terraces, cottages and villas. To number 257 the Latham family moved until 1906 when they moved up the road to number 365. My great grandfather Frederick Dudley Latham was born in 1878 and married Esther Masters whose uncle was John Humble. For dedicated Arsenal supporters, John was a major influence at Woolwich Arsenal. For many years he was the club's secretary, chairman and director. At the age of 18 he walked to London from Durham, found a job at the Arsenal and became one of the 15 founders and Beardsley's understudy in goal. Largely responsible for recording the early details of the club, it was Humble who took Arsenal into the professional ranks of the League and who, after Chapman and Norris, must be regarded as the most important figure in Arsenal's history. Humble remained a director until a scandal in 1927 forced him, though wholly innocent, to resign. Sir Henry Norris sold the team bus and the money had somehow appeared in his wife's bank account. His response was it was repayment for money he paid to bring Charlie Buchan to Highbury in 1925. He was eventually drummed out of the game taking Humble with him.

Fred, when he married was a very competent amateur boxer and John introduced him to the sport of football. He turned out on several occasions for Woolwich Arsenal and was awarded 3 whiteskull caps with the Arsenal motif on it picked out in a dark blue. These caps had a tassel on it of gold and dark blue silk for these appearances. However, these were destroyed by his second wife when he died in

1942 in a bitter feud between herself and my grandfather. The appearances were as A N Other or trialist as the club records do not have him listed under his name. The club Historian Mr Bevan went to great length's in the 1980's to provide this information for me. My grandfather also called Fred Dudley Latham knew a lot of people who remember him playing at inside right. Unfortunately they are all now dead including my grandfather so getting further information now is impossible. I have always wondered if any other examples of these caps remain in existence now! Fred senior had another relative who played for Royal and Woolwich Arsenal but unfortunately I have no information on him.

Fred was also a member of the City of London Yeomanry and was the first person in the regiment to be awarded the King Edward VIIth Territorial Force Efficiency Medal in April 1909 with a further clasp awarded in 1936. I have a lot of photographs of him in uniform most of which copies were made and given to the regiments museum as all their information was lost during a fire during the blitz in world war two. He was a Trumpeter Major a similar rank to a warrant officer these days. I have inherited his 1914-15 Star war medal but not the other three which were believed stolen in the 1950's. Also a sword which he took from a Turkish officer at Gallipoli and his swagger stick. A very proud man who loved organising. This was further proved after the war when he returned and moved to Chalfont St Peter in Buckinghamshire. He designed and built his own house on Gold Hill common a couple of houses down from the Jolly Farmer Pub. The house was mostly constructed from pure cement. I hate to think what happened when electricians tried to chase the walls to install electricity! The house still stands today and because of the way it was constructed probably will remain for many years to come!

He became a Mason and fairly high ranking in the order of the Buffalo. Because of his football past he was approached in 1926 to start up a local football side. He accepted and Chalfont St Peter FC was formed. They still play at the Playing Fields as a semi professional side in the ICIS League. Fred played a few games with

2

his brother George but not many because of his age. He died on 15th June 1942 at Westminster Hospital following a heart attack on Liverpool Street Station.

His brother George Dudley Latham was very close to Fred and also took up football. He was born in Woolwich and became an electrician by trade. George was chief electrical engineer at the Rock Film Studios, Hastings and when the Gaiety Theatre, Hastings was converted into a cinema, he was in charge of the electrical installation. Whilst living in Woolwich he played football for Charlton Athletic at inside right- the same position as brother Fred! He played throughout 1913 - 14 season and would have had a longer career had the first world war not broken out. For the duration of the war he worked at the Arsenal before joining Fred at Chalfont St Peter. He played for Chalfont for several seasons before moving to Hastings, where he became a member of a prominent London Lodge of Freemasons. In 1941 he became the licensee of the Stag Inn, in Saints Street, Hastings. His brother Fred was coming to visit him when he had his heart attack on the station platform. George was grief stricken and died at the age of 50 three months later.

The two brothers started a family tradition of supporting Arsenal and Charlton which continues to this day.

Fred Junior avidly supported the Gunners and frequently went to Highbury when he was working in London. When he wasn't he would watch Chalfont play. I have fond memories of him sitting in the stand watching the games until his death a couple of years ago. His last request was to have a party in Chalfont's club house and let all his friends have one last drink on him. This was carried out to the letter. It was the last time I visited the club!

Fred Junior had two sons Tony and my father Dudley (of course - this name continues as a family name as it is also my middle name. However, it stopped with me as my ex wife refused to include it in my son's name when he was born much to the disgust of my grandfather!). Dudley carried on with the football tradition as Tony decided not to take any involvement. From when he was born in 1940 he had "Red" blood in him and supported Arsenal. He played for his school and his county, Buckinghamshire alongside a few famous players including Mike Keen, who went on to play for QPR, Watford and Luton. He later opened a sports shop in High Wycombe and managed Wycombe Wanderers. His son Kevin is still in the game at Stoke City! His success led to trials with Arsenal. I still have his two postcards signed by George Male the then Arsenal manager inviting him to have the trials. The first was at Highbury on Thursday 9th May 1957 at 6.30pm. He scored a "cracking goal" as my late grandfather described it and was awarded a second trial on Tuesday 13th August 1957 at Grovelands Ground, Southgate. Unfortunately the worry of school exams and a touch of flu played their part and he was unsuccessful. As a result of that day's trial a certain talented left back called John Sanchez was discovered and signed. Although he didn't make the grade at least he can say he played and scored for an Arsenal XI! shortly afterwards a cartilage operation restricted his playing and he gave up playing after continuing the other family tradition of playing for Chalfont St Peter in 1958. He married in 1963 to Patricia Buckman and I came along on the 2nd April 1965.

My mother's family was less football oriented, but still living in Chalfont the club had an influence. My aunt Eileen married Chris Birch, who played a bit. He had unsuccessful trials at Watford then played for Chalfont in the late sixties. Having moved up the road to Stoke Poges his career was finished on the parks playing for Hedgeley in the Sunday League. In fact my mothers side was more film related! Her dad was also called Fred and lived in Chalfont. He worked at Rank Film studios in Denham. When he joined up in the second world war, the film studios bought him out of the army to concentrate on making films for the war effort. He remained with Rank until his retirement. He never followed senior football but loved to watch the schoolboy internationals on TV. I was very close to him and his death still haunts me. I was due to go over and see both him and my grandmother in 1987 when I was working close by in Slough. A problem occurred and I had to work late so didn't go. On getting home to my fiancee at the time I learnt he had had a heart attack and died. If I had gone I would have been there to see him alive and say goodbye to him properly when he died. He missed my marriage a few months later and seeing my two children. It is something I will always regret and will stay with me for the rest of my life!

Chris was also in the film industry. Being a company accountant he worked for Hemdale films a small company owned by actor David Hemmings. I used to have a lot of fun looking round the film studios and would have appeared in an advert for Space Dust a popular sweet at the time had I been a bit smaller. As the last time I visited they were filming the advert for American TV and one person had dropped out. Still the film Premieres were good!

The rest of my mothers side of the family had military backgrounds. Her uncle Walter was in the Coldstream Guards then an Inspector in the Palestine Police before and during the second world war. Cousin Jim Sparks was in the RAF as a pilot who spent most of his time training airmen in Africa. Walter Sparks was killed during the first world war whilst serving with the Royal Artillery during the siege of Kut Al Amara which is now in Iraq. Walter Starling was also a casualty killed in France whilst serving with the 2nd Battalion Northumberland Fusiliers. My mothers family originate from the Blyth/ Morpeth area near Newcastle and the Sandringham area in Norfolk. In fact my grandmothers mother is according to family tradition the illegitimate daughter of King Edward VII, as her grandmother was in service at Sandringham. I tried to research this as have several other members of my family but a cover up was implemented by the royal family (nothing changes even then!) and a lot of money comes into the family which lasted until my great aunt Margaret died in Canada in the late 80's and I received part of the estate. No firm evidence was found such was the cover up so it is down to hear say and word of mouth. If it was true as the money no doubt confirmed then I have royal blood in me. Not that it will do me any good as with all the other troubles the Queen currently has I'm sure this would only add to it. And I have no way of proving anything let alone wanting a stake in the royal family.

Two years after I was born my brother Paul came along. He never showed any interest in Sport what so ever. Hopefully I made up for it, and my son Christopher is also following in that tradition preferring to play in goal.

Chapter 2
The Early Days

My first introduction to something which would take over my life for a few years - football came about in 1976. My dad was watching the Southampton v Manchester United FA Cup Final on TV. As we were living in Yateley at the time, we had three local sides Aldershot Town, Reading and Southampton. As this was the Saints finest hour my dad was cheering them on and I suddenly took an interest in the game and watched most of the match. That was it I was hooked! I started to play it in the garden with my friends and in the fields behind our road. My parents then introduced me to subbuteo which all the other kids in Lodge Grove had. We set up our own league and played in each others houses. I was Arsenal and took my team with me to "away matches" next door. To start with I was thrashed regularly especially by the older kids, but with time and practise I got better. I then started Senior School - Yateley Comprehensive. The school team colours were red shirts and blue shorts the same as Aldershot played in. I tried very hard to get into the school team but my inexperience and the fact that I was smaller, fatter and less mobile than them proved a deciding factor. I even tried out for the school cricket team during the summer term but failed to make any progress for the same reasons.

May 1977 I remember fondly for being allowed to stay up late to watch the European Cup Final between Liverpool and Borussia Monchengladbach That match made me want to see a match live and my dad promised me he would take me to see Aldershot play Arsenal in a friendly in August. June arrived and Dudley was promoted to Finished Products Manager at United Glass in Alloa. We all flew up and stayed at the Powfowlis Manor Hotel near Larbert whilst looking for a place to live. This period was the longest I could remember being with my father. He worked hard at United Glass's Head Office in Staines so when he got home I was in bed, Saturday was a routine of shopping then going to buy fresh bread from a bakers by Crowthorne station. The afternoon dad was around but on Sundays he was at Golf, being a member of Frimley Park Golf Club. He was never around to watch me grow up. Only for the smackings when Paul and I were naughty. So I enjoyed trying to get to know him properly. The thrill of flying for the first time going to a new country then being able to watch a beacon light being lit on the Ochil Hills to celebrate the Queen's Silver Jubilee made the week very exciting and I looked forward to the move. We found a house, well it was more like a mansion compared to what we were used to living in. St John's Rectory in Grange Road. A large house with a large garden backing onto a local park. The front looked out onto a nursery and the glassworks where dad was to work. It was perfect! We returned home and put the house in Yateley on the market. Things moved pretty quickly and a moving date was set. Then horror of horrors the date we were to move was the date of the Aldershot friendly. I pleaded with my parents to put back the move by 24 hours so I could go. They refused and let me down. I was very upset at being let down.

"It is only a football match"

was my dads response. But it was special not only was it my first match but it featured Arsenal and I was going to miss it. We travelled up to Scotland on the train and all I could think of was being let down and wondering what the score was at the game. I hardly spoke to my parents that evening.

Once we had moved in I had only a couple of days to get used to the place before school started. Alloa Academy was split into two buildings. The first two years were spent at the annex in Grange Road only 100 yards from the house. I started school not knowing anyone and feeling very miserable. I even had a bird flying overhead deposit droppings on my head during break time. I had a bad first day not many people wanted to talk to me let alone make friends. I felt totally alone and abandoned. I had to put up with taunts and jibes because I was English and a stranger.

I was never sure on how guilty my father felt about missing the Aldershot match but he tried to make amends. Alloa Athletic had just been promoted as runners-up in the Scottish Second Division and were to start their first ever season in the First Division (the leagues were expanded in 1975). Their first ever match was against Arbroath on 13th August and dad took me along. The game finished in a 1 - 1 draw and I can't really remember it as I was busy taking in the atmosphere, the old wooden stand, bridies and Bovril at half time. But I wanted more and I was taken to 17 games that season. I kept a record of every game and it started a trend where I keep the records going to this day. What an anorak, still at least it is better than train spotting!

The following week at school I made known I enjoyed football and it helped break the ice and I started making friends. The Scottish syllabus is different to that taught in England so I had to readjust. It became apparent why I was not accepted readily when I studied history. In England I was taught about ancient romans, stone age man etc., in Scotland it was Scottish history which was very much church of Scotland driven. For the two years studies before I dropped it in favour of geography I had Archie Knox and the Prespeterian Church driven into me at regular intervals and about Bannockburn, which was only a few miles up the road. Most of the history was about how badly the English had treated the Scots in the past. The English had made mistakes in history and the Scots do not let themselves forget about it.

Ireland has the troubles because of similar teachings. They are taught from an early age so both the Catholics and Protestants hate each other to the point of fighting. Fortunately the Scots are not that extreme, but in some parts of the country the hatred they have for the English is really noticeable. Tourists don't notice it but anyone living their will experience it. If countries can't forget the past and continue to live in it then hatred will always exist. Having said that once I was accepted at school I was left alone and although taunts were made especially when Scotland played England in the Home International Championships and they failed to qualify for the 1978 world cup finals in Argentina. I found some very good friends in Alloa who became very loyal.

One day after sports I noticed my watch had been stolen. The thief was found and given the belt. I had to be hauled in front of the headmaster and told to calm down my friends who had openly threatened the thief with further punishment for stealing from me. I was flattered that I was cared about given the poor reception I had experienced not two months previously.

My second football match followed on 28th September when I was taken to see Heart of Midlothian (Hearts) play Alloa my first experience of a big club and Tynecastle was a big ground. Dad found a friendly turnstile operator who was only too happy to let a certain 12 year old hop over the turnstile and get in free whilst dad only paid for himself. The game proved to be a good one with Alloa losing 1 - 0 and going to the bottom of the league, something which they would do for most of the season.

By this time dad had found another golf club ShawPark in Sauchie and had made a few friends. One of whom happened to be the father of Alan and John Hansen. Alan had just transferred from Partick Thistle to Liverpool for £100, 000 and was struggling to get into the team. Brother John was an ex Partick and Scotland player who had retired early due to injury and was working for the Abbey National Building Society. I was to get to know them well over the next few years!

Friday nights was golf club drinks night and dad always seemed to win on the fruit machines because he would come home late with a Chinese meal most nights and wake me with a spare rib. At long last my father was taking a real interest in me.

December brought a couple more games at the Recreation Park, but 1978 I was allowed out to more matches and made the most of it. January I recall vividly as the first match of the new year was a 5 - 0 thrashing by Morton the game was forgetful but I remember meeting a very arrogant big head called Mark McGhee who pushed past me on his way to the dressing room Nothing changes there! The 29th brought gales to Scotland and I fondly remember the Scottish Cup 3rd Round match against Dumbarton for an event I doubt I will ever see again. The Alloa goalkeeper Dougie McNab took a goal kick from the Clackmannan Road end, the ball reached the half way line at a reasonable height when a gust of wind caught the ball and sent it back over Doug's head for a corner. Despite the conditions the game finished in a 2 - 2 draw.

As a treat one of dads golf friends got tickets for the 4th round cup game between Rangers and Stirling Albion. Although Stirling are to Alloa as Tottenham is to Arsenal we still went along Ibrox was impressive even then before all the redevelopment I couldn't help but be impressed.

The reason that crowds in the Scottish League are poor is due to location, all the main clubs are within an hours drive of each other if you forget the outposts of Dumfries and Aberdeen, so the main following is for Rangers and Celtic. Even in Alloa I knew of three different supporters clubs in the town who took coach loads of fans to the games. At times it would have been quicker to announce crowd changes to the teams rather than the other way round. Alloa averaged 1, 000 crowds that season, it would go down to about 500 in the lower league when they were relegated. This was common with most clubs. Exceptions being Ross County and Inverness Caledonian Thistle as they are too far away from Glasgow so can hold a big catchment area to pull in supporters.

From the visit to Ibrox to the end of the season I went to every home game and two further trips to Tynecastle. I only missed one home match because of a holiday to England for a week I was now firmly addicted to the game.

The trip to England was a long tiring one. Stagecoach had just started up and were no where near as good as they were then. The trip was one of their first in an old uncomfortable coach with lunch being provided. I still remember a soggy sandwich and a dry piece of cake wrapped in cling film being handed to me. Tea was via several flasks of hot water. Its weird how you tend to remember the odd things in life!

Dad stayed up in Scotland to work and as mum's attempts to learn to drive had nearly written off dads car we were reliant on my grandfather and my uncle to take us around. Chris made up for dads error at the start of the season by taking me to see a football league match. Standing on the terraces at Griffin Park watching Brentford beat Barnsley 2 - 0 in a 4th Division match was not my ideal game but it was the nearest and I was grateful for him taking me. A couple of days later just prior to enduring the return journey up north I went to watch Chalfont St Peter play Marlow in the Athenian League. My other Grandfather was sat in the stand and was completely surprised to see me as mum hadn't told him we were coming down. My first experience of my families club was very friendly. I was introduced to everyone in the ground. Then again given the clubs history explained in chapter one and the fact that my family had lived in the town for 60 years everyone knew us. The club Secretary David Puttnam made me feel very important and he was interested in the Scottish League and we kept in touch for years to come, even when he moved to Fleet and took over control of Fleet Town.

Back up North the season was played out and Alloa were sent back from whence they came to the second division. The season finished with an all stars charity match at the Patons & Baldwins sports ground. This was the first of an annual series of matches in which a lot of big stars appeared. I was to get involved with this at a later date!

At about this time I started my growth spurt ahead of all my fellow classmates which was to my advantage as the weight dropped off and rather than confining my skills to a subbuteo pitch found I was able to excel in sports. My speed picked up and the summer term took everyone by surprise when I was selected in Athletics to run not only for the school team but for the county on one occasion. This honour led to my captaining the school team. This got me noticed and I even ended up meeting Alan Hansen when the school was playing a match against his old school - Lornshill Academy. I had a long chat with him which had some effect for the start of the following football season my dad came back from his golf club on a Friday night with a signed annual, photo and autograph book full of the Liverpool teams signatures. Alan had decided to do something without being asked and as he knew dad made an effort to make a young teenager very happy. He succeeded! I became a bit of a fan and followed his career. We kept in touch whilst he was living in club digs at 10 Trap Hill, Formby, but when he moved after marrying Janet we lost touch. Now his career is over it is nice to know he is still involved with football even if it is as a TV pundit.

Alloa Academy didn't have a football team, instead they concentrated on Rugby so I gave it ago and to my surprise I enjoyed it. I started playing in an inter school 7 a side tournament in Alva. The end result caught me by surprise. I was put in as a flanker as my speed was good and as a result I was noticed by a scout who was in attendance to watch some public schoolboys from Queen Victoria High School in Dunblane. I was asked to try out for Scotland Schoolboys which I readily accepted. Unfortunately I was unsuccessful in the trials but at least I got to have a go. I found as the months went on I gained experience and became an ever present in the school side and played for the county and for the Central Region twice. My organisational skills were recognised by Jim Stalker the school Geography teacher who put me in charge of keeping the school results and fixtures. Other than myself there were only three others who were in the team all season: Eric Revie; Paul Robertson and Gary Bryce. All three continued their playing careers in rugby after leaving school and played in the Scottish League. Gary becoming a star at Alloa Rugby Club. I scored three tries during the season, in a rather dire season for the school.

The football season kicked off with Stirling playing a friendly with Port Vale. I had a guest with me called Tony Incenzo who was travelling round all the Scottish grounds having just completed all 92 English grounds and finishing off with a TV appearance on Noel Edmonds Swap Shop. Tony was a bit self opinionated but otherwise a nice guy. We had an arrangement that if I was in London and QPR were playing I would go with him using his mother's season ticket. I took him up on the offer a few seasons later. I believe he is working behind the scenes now at Loftus Road. This game was followed by visits of Hartlepool and Bradford City to Alloa. This time in the football season is my favourite as I get to see different clubs playing and view possible upsets that wouldn't otherwise occur. The weather is better which also helps! Bradford were full of ex Leeds stars from their glory days headed by Paul Madeley so it was a treat to watch the stars cruise past Alloa 3 - 1. I had two real highlights of the season. One at the start and one at the end. I actually got to see Arsenal play! They came up to play Celtic in a friendly at Parkhead and fielded a full strength team including Malcolm MacDonald who scored in the 3 - 0 win. Dad was now vindicated for his error last year. He took me to a few away matches that year and to see Hearts play Aberdeen in their first game back in the Premier League but backed away from the home games as he had other things to do on a Saturday. So I went on my own, to most of the 40 games I attended that season. A couple of away games I went with school friends. One Steven Lawlor has an uncle Pat who is still a director at the club, but his dad drove an open pickup truck so on several occasions we sat out in the open in the back driving up to Stirling and Dunfermline. Quite what the police would have said is another matter, but then again I knew the local traffic policeman and had ago on the back of his police bike which was against police regulations, so I doubt if anything would have been said.

The second highlight was on 21st April when my parents confirmed that they would buy me a season ticket for the Recs. for next season, this was followed up by a terrific match against East Fife. The wasps won 4 - 3 thanks to the strangest goal. Lindsay Hamilton had just joined Alloa and was keen to make an impression. Alloa were awarded an indirect free kick on the halfway line just in front of the stand. The weather was lovely and hot (strange for Scotland!) and no wind. He belted the ball at the goalkeeper who rather than let it go panicked and went for it touching it as it went in for the winning goal.

The season then finished with the now annual charity match at Patons more stars turned up and it was a success.

1979-80 season saw a lot of changes. Firstly I moved up to the main annex at the Academy walking up Redwell Place in the winter was to be an event in itself a very steep hill which once the snow and ice appeared made walking impossible.

This was to be my last season playing rugby. I was being picked out by the schools we were playing against as they were used to us and our tactics. We had the obligatory stuffing by the Queen Victoria High in Dunblane this time it was 68 - 4. But as the school was made up of officers sons who spend a lot of their free time playing the sport, they thrashed most of the local sides out of sight. I picked up numerous injuries including against Alva a seriously cut head when I was stamped on deliberately whilst in a collapsed scrum which involved a visit to the hospital. Enough was enough and I didn't see the need to deliberately injure the opposition to win. I hung up my boots.

Life at Alloa Athletic took a turn for the better which meant the season ticket that I now proudly owned was not needed, but I will deal with that in Chapter three.

1980 saw the school give in to pupil pressure and one of the maths teachers Ian Young started up a football team. I was more than happy to play. We were thrashed regularly, but looking at the opposition DCL Distillers an adult Sunday league side it was hardly surprising, yet it proved to strengthen the team for seasons to come in the Scottish League. I started out in midfield but preferred a centre forwards role. The end result came about by accident. A goalkeeping crisis occurred and I was put in goal. I remained reserve keeper for the rest of the season when not required up field. A school colleague was studying photography and took some shots of me in goal to embarrass me. It succeeded! We played against some good sides and looking back it is surprising to see who went further in their careers. John Sludden and Paul McStay went to Celtic whilst Joe Tortalano went to Hibernian. Ally Dick went down south to join Tottenham Hotspur, Hugh Stevenson went to Dumbarton; John McCormack to Falkirk. Of the Academy side: David Cooper and myself went to Alloa Athletic; Douglas Lawrie went to Hibernian, Hamilton, Airdrie, Stirling Albion

15

before arriving at Alloa. He also was fortunate to play for Scotland at schoolboy level. A match I went to watch at the expense of watching the Wasps playing Stranraer at the Rec.'s - the only match I missed all season! Also in the team was Derek Jackson who played in goal for many seasons at Arbroath, Trevor Smith who went onto Dunfermline and Tony Hill who went onto captain Arbroath via Hibernian. And John Cousin who went to Stirling Albion.

My parents have fond memories of Trevor Smith who was last seen throwing up all over my mums flowers in the back garden after a Christmas party. His dad George was an ex Scotland and Dunfermline player, but now Head of Alva Academy. He took a very dim view of that evenings events, but that is another story!

Above: me in goal against DCL Distillers. Far right the referee is George Smith the ex Dunfermline and Scotland player. Father of Trevor.
Below: A team photo from Alloa Academy missing are Douglas Lawrie and Trevor Smith. To my left is Tony Hill and Derek Jackson whilst in front is John Cousin.

Chapter 3
A Lucky Break

Our local newsagent, George Ormiston, was also the secretary at Alloa FC! At the start of 1979-80 season the position of Programme Editor became available at the club. The old editor Jim Carswell had to step down to concentrate on his business a local drapers store in Sauchie. The previous season had finished with me helping him look after some guests at Hampden Park when the wasps played there. I supervised the youngsters during a tour of the ground so had become noticed within the club. I approached George who was sceptical about a schoolboy taking over a responsible position. At that time a local supporter called Sam Harris offered to do the job, so it was agreed he would take overall responsibility for printing etc. and the pair of us would look after the editorial. This brought a mixed reaction from my parents, having just purchased a season ticket for me it was now obsolete as being an official I was automatically given free admission to all matches.

Due to internal politics over production costs the programme was not issued until the end of October for the visit of Stenhousemuir, a pity really as the club missed out on issuing for several big matches which would have meant good sales, as opposed to the subsidised version from the previous year.

The season got off to the perfect start. Following draws with Bradford City and Motherwell it was straight into league action at home to Brechin City. What a match to start with. An entertaining first half finished 3 a piece, but the second half was a different story when Alloa stepped up a gear and walked through the men from Glebe Park to stroll home comfortable 8 - 3 winners. Praise for the victory fell on my friend and personal mentor Hugh Wilson, the manager. Hugh Wilson was a great personality at the club. A miner by trade and having had a lot of success with other clubs had continued it with Alloa guiding them to promotion a couple of seasons ago. He was later sacked and moved on to Cowdenbeath a former club of his. When he died a couple of years ago the event was mentioned on teletext, Such was his popularity. A sad loss to Scottish Football! I will always remember his happy smiling face he always had time to stop and have a chat. I needed some information for the programme and attended training one evening, that was the start of a great friendship. He spend time with me whilst Alex Totten the coach took the training session. I got all I needed and Hugh always made time for me every week to praise my efforts and give items for inclusion in the programme. Had it not been for his encouragement I probably wouldn't have gone as far as I had in the game.

The 8 - 3 victory proved to be the highlight of the season, from then on the club nose-dived and had the embarrassment of finishing bottom of the second division. Hugh was sacked and Alex took over for his first managerial position. All round it was a disappointing season for the club. George Ormiston suffered personal heartache when his elder brother Robert died. He had fought during the 1st World War and been a member of the club since 1946 when he became a director. For myself it was hectic, but brought personal rewards!

After going to Stirling on the back of the truck with Steven to watch Celtic beat Albion 2 -1 in the league cup, a comment was raised by Steven that his uncle Pat had received a lot of grief from supporters on account of the directors not issuing programmes or celebrating the club's centenary in 1978 as they felt it occurred in 1983. This sparked something off in me and I went to the library to investigate. The result was three hours every Thursday for three seasons in the Library studying old newspapers on microfilm. The facts I retrieved were used in the programme and was a great success with the fans. It turned out that the club was founded in 1878, but they did not join the Scottish Football Association until 1883, hence the mix up.

Not only was I writing the programme, and organising the programme sellers, but I was on the committee of the supporters club and helped clean up the ground after the matches. This did not go un noticed as I later found out. On 1st December Forfar Athletic were the visitors. The team bus arrived outside the ground were I was standing telling the programme sellers were to position themselves. I said hello to one of the players as they went in. Later I dropped into the away dressing room with their complementary copies of the programme. A voice cried out

"Back again".

It was the player I had spoken to earlier. After the match I was in front of the dug outs tidying up some litter when the team emerged. I heard a laugh and some people approaching me. One was Alex Rae one of Forfar's star players noticeable by his silver hair and moustache. He asked me what didn't I do at the club. To which my response was "not much!"

Every time they visited or I travelled up to Station Park he made a point of finding me, and having a quick chat. I later learnt that he had approached Mackinlay's and the Scottish League and nominated me for Personality of the Month award. Unfortunately apart from the glory of the coveted award the prize was a bottle of Scotch donated by Mackinlay's and being under 18 I was not allowed to receive anything illegal. The award went to an unknown Aberdeen manager called Alex Ferguson. I wonder what ever happened to him? Hugh was the only person from the club honoured by Mackinlay's when he was runner up in April 1977 having gained promotion for the club. The gesture had not gone un noticed and if I ever see Alex again I will be sure to buy him a drink. Mackinlay's also sponsored a book called the A - Z of Scottish Football. the first edition left a lot out about the second division and I received a letter from its author Forrest Robertson, asking for assistance the resulting second edition was about twice the size of the first and correct with all the facts I had supplied.

The season saw me do a little training with the club and Hugh let me have a few minutes playing for them during a close door friendly with local amateur side Boness United. We lost 3-1, but that was the most exciting moment of my career. My first appearance for a senior club! On the park the club's slide down the division was rapid by the end of the year. However, they were drawn at home to play Hearts in the Scottish Cup 3rd Round. Hearts were flying high in the Premier League and came with a full squad. Alloa played them off the park! They were winning 1 - 0 when thick fog descended around the ground. The game was then abandoned after 50 minutes. The weather had come to Hearts' rescue. Having been saved they were prewarned as to the tactics used by Hugh and responded by providing a very entertaining match which they just won 1 - 0. A couple of weeks later the Supporter's club held their annual draw. I was drawn second out of the hat and won the sum of £3. Given that the programmes were only 10p at the time it seemed like a lot of money then. Mind you there were a few shouts of

"Fix"

from amongst the supporters.

Away games were now very affordable for me as I had free travel on the team bus and complimentary tickets thrown in. On the team coach, we had an unwritten rule of segregation the players kept themselves to themselves with their card school on the tables in the centre of the coach, Hugh McCann winning more than he should on the longer trips. I actually did my homework on the back seat to the amusement of some of the squad. Whilst the front end was the "Royal Box" reserved for Management and Directors. This was the quietest end going to the grounds, but quite often the noisiest during the return journey after the directors had been well looked after in the opposing home team's drinks cabinet/boardroom before and after the match. The journey home was normally the point after matches when expense claims were submitted by the players whilst the senior members of the board were jolly I can't imagine why!

Doug McNab was a school teacher and took a lot of interest in my studies on the team bus between card games, I missed him when he was transferred to Partick Thistle. My closest friends became Alan Holt and his fiancee, later wife Karen Gray, and Lindsay Hamilton. Lindsay enjoyed telling the story of his goal against East Fife and although the rest of the team were by now bored to death over it I took an interest. He loved to be popular and when given a player profile to fill out for the programme, he was the first of the team to return it completed. He always described himself as a civil servant, however in reality he was the local tax inspector. I threatened to change his profile when I found out, but Karen warned me that he had investigated a few locals for tax evasion and to disclose his job would make him very unpopular on the terraces. I relented. I kept in touch with the three of them for a few years after leaving the club. One addition to the squad was Lex Shields, who had signed from Boness having impressed during the close door friendly. Then the "Old Man" arrived. Gregor Abel, we had met on numerous times before. He was a teacher in Larbert and was first on the scene when I had my head stamped on in the rugby match described in the previous chapter. His experience helped stop the rot and a few good results were put together. Gregor stayed with the club for several seasons qualifying with SFA Coaching badges, he later became the club's coach and manager.

Dougie McNab was recognised along with Hugh McCann and both played for the Scotland under 21 side. This got Doug noticed and his departure was immanent, when Partick stepped in to sign him it was the final nail in the club's coffin for the season. Having no back up keeper Hugh panicked and brought in a local lad called Stan Drummond from amateur side Broxburn. He came on a months loan and made his debut away to Brechin on 1st March. He was outstanding and Alloa fought to achieve a precious point in a 1 - 1 draw. However, once signed his performances dropped and I made it plain that even I could do better than him. At that point Hugh put me in goal for 5 a sides at training, but stayed loyal to Stan. As a person Stan was terrific, but he was so inconsistent and became subject to abuse from the terraces for producing spectacular saves but letting in soft goals.

With the side now rooted to the foot of the division attendance's became lower to the point were the club were losing money. The directors took a serious look at budgets, and following the match with Albion Rovers on 15th March decided not issue any further

programmes for the remainder of the season. Sam Harris at this point
was fed up with the club and left, leaving me with sole responsibility
for a non existent programme.

Alan became the Supporters Club Player of the Year, and I was one
of the first to congratulate him. It was the only positive thing to
happen throughout April and May. Following a humiliating 4 - 1
defeat at home to Brechin who fielded the same side that lost 8 - 3 at
the start of the season, I took a week off as there was no programme
to produce and headed down south. The break did me a lot of good
and for a birthday present, Chris took me to Highbury for my first visit
to see Arsenal play a 1 - 1 draw with Southampton. Alan Sunderland
scored, but I spent most of my time watching my heroes Pat Jennings,
Frank Stapleton and Liam Brady performing for their fan clubs. The
return was long as usual. On arriving in Alloa I had to turn round and
head back south as Alloa were playing at Stranraer the following day.
The team bus normally collected me from my house as it was stored
by the glassworks. This time it didn't so dad quickly drove me to the
ground. I was greeted by stunned looks from the officials, who let me
on the coach without saying a word. On the journey down the physio
Fred Rae came up to me and inquired where I would be sleeping that
night?
"In the hotel with the players as normal"
was my reply. It was then explained to me that as I had been away and
not due back till late the club hadn't booked me a room in the hotel.
On arriving at the hotel they were found to be fully booked, so I
slipped away from the evening meal to find a bed and breakfast
establishment. Fortunately because of the Larne ferry terminal nearby
bed and breakfast places were plentiful and I quickly found
somewhere to bed down for the night. It took along while for me to
live that experience down. The following morning I wondered around
sight seeing not that there was much to see in Stranraer! before joining
the players at the hotel for lunch. The whole trip was a disaster as the
coach driver smashed the coach into the entrance gates to Stair Park.
(The ground is situated in the middle of a public Recreation Park). A

local nutter from the local hospital had used my name to get a complimentary ticket right next to me. He then spent the whole match taking endlessly about something which I was trying to avoid listening to. This was then capped off by him spilling tea over my suit at half time in the board room. The team then did their usual thing ably assisted by Stan playing one of his blinders in goal again by losing 4 - 0. The eventful weekend was then finished by the team stopping off near Kilmarnock on the way home for fish and chips. My soggy trousers had just about dried off when they were treated to a further soaking with grease as our leading goalkeeper went for the coachrail getting onto the bus and missed. His chips flew into the air, he went to catch them and missed. They landed on me following behind him.

A fortnight later we returned down south to Dumfries to play Queen of the South, perhaps fearing the worst after the Stranraer trip the directors decided to go and come back on the same day. This was the last away game of the season and the club could go no higher than bottom so the pressure was off and following a 0 - 0 draw we made our way home in a carnival type of atmosphere having gained our first away point for about 6 weeks. Queens Park finished the season off by winning 1 -0 and Hugh Wilson was sacked by the board of directors. This took the shine off the all stars charity match the following week which was now being run by the Alloa & District Festival Committee.

Chapter 4
The Only Way is Up

My mother hates football, yet she entered a rebellious stage for the next couple of years! This all started when she was listening to a Phone in Programme on Radio Forth. The Disc Jockey was slating the English and this provoked her into picking the phone up and openly argue with him on a few nationalist points over the air. I'm not sure what this did to his ratings but she became popular and featured on the programme fairly regularly after that. I seem to remember the DJ's name being Tom Bell, who sent her a signed photo. Not content with her moment of fame she let off steam at the way the Alloa & District Festival Committee had made a few mistakes when organising the previous years event. The response was

"put your money where your mouth is",

so she joined the festival committee and helped organise the local Beauty Contest and then got involved with a gentleman named Murdo McGregor who had been organising the annual Charity football matches. Between them they attempted to make it more professional by staging this years event as Alloa FC v the All Stars. The Scottish League and Football Association took a very dim view of this and banned Alloa players from taking part in a match against a non registered side, however they did not drop this bomb shell until a few weeks before the end of the season and threw the event organisers into a state of confusion. The problem was got around I guested for the team representing Alloa as I was not a "signed" player. The all stars were doubled and the match was All Stars v All Stars, resulting in a 6 - 5 win for the team I was on. Returning for his third year was John Hansen, ably assisted by Pat Crerand; Willie Morgan; Dennis Law, Joe Baker and Jim Baxter, in fact looking back I was the only non international playing for the team. The charity match was a success, although a thief broke into the changing room after the match and stole my football boots along with Willie Morgan's Scotland Cap which had been brought along for display use, whilst we were all enjoying a buffet tea.

1980 - 81 season kicked off with Alex Totten in charge. He was quite a culture shock from Hugh, although we all knew him, This Area Sales Manager who had started his playing career at Liverpool, before going onto Dundee, Dunfermline, Falkirk and Queen of the South, was an extremely ambitious man. He wanted success to further his managerial career and made that plain to everyone. Underneath this harsh front was a very caring family man who was married to Jessie and had two kids whom he adored Bruce and Kay. He had won medals playing for every team except Queen of the South and wanted this success to continue from day one in the hot seat. This led to a volatile friendship between the two of us, as normally when I spoke to him it was as he was preparing himself for a team talk or just after a match when he was never in the best of moods. However, success did come his way and I still watch him appear on Sky TV on Tartan Extra as manager of Premier League side Kilmarnock.

I was now responsible for the entire programme production as well as training with the team, researching at the library all whilst fitting in with my school work. Quite how I finished with 7 O levels is beyond me! Task one was a failure persuading the directors to produce a quality programme on 16 pages instead of 12. Budgets warranted otherwise so I had to put up and shut up. Having said that George Ormiston tried his best to fight my corner with the directors, but at least they said yes to production again, after last seasons demise. This led to my first commercial decision. I promised the directors if they allowed me to put up the price of the programme by 50% to 15p the profit made would then be split between the club and improving the issue to make it acceptable with the boo boys on the terraces. They agreed, so I changed the cover to incorporate a photo changeable with every issue. This met with universal praise. One of the players lived near Coatbridge so we arranged for him to collect the programmes rather than pay to have them delivered. These savings allowed for the budget to include costs for the full season's production. The fans would not be sold short this year. However, in doing this I had to agree that the first issue would be a double issue to incorporate the Clyde game on 6th September and Forfar the following Tuesday. It was felt and later justified by the attendance that Forfar would not bring many supporters down for a mid week game and so sales would be poor. By making this the first issue they missed out the home games with Rangers (friendly); Cowdenbeath (league); and Hibernian (League Cup). A local derby and two top Premier sides. Profits would have been made and I had produced a programme for each game only to have production stopped by those in the board room. This upset Alex Totten, who following the 2 - 0 defeat with Hibs promptly sided with me and put pressure on the directors to not meddle which they promptly agreed to. The team beat Clyde 2 - 0 to go to the top of the league. The atmosphere changed around the ground, gone was the dispair of last year instead their was hope and excitement on the terraces. I was reappointed onto the committee of the supporters club although much to the annoyance of my committee members stopped helping to clear up after the game. I had enough responsibilities without that and made my feelings known. If it was not accepted I was prepared to resign. They accepted and the Supporters Club and myself had a peaceful and harmonious relationship for the rest of the season.

Alan Hansen was now establishing himself in the first team at Anfield so his visits were less frequent. He supplied me with the new seasons team autographs and annual without asking. He sent it to his brother John who delivered it one night on the way home from work. John had just been promoted to Director level within the Abbey National Building Society, so other than the end of season charity match, that was the last time I would see him!

My programme stats were producing interest throughout the other League clubs. My research at the library had started in 1878 and worked forward, so I was starting to supply teams, results and information from Alloa's first meetings with other sides. I was getting quite a name for myself outside of Clackmannanshire. I started doing freelance journalism in my spare time promoting the Scottish League and very quickly started getting a lot of correspondence from throughout the United Kingdom. But it didn't stop there as letters arrived from Canada, West Germany, Holland and Sweden. The Swedish one was from a gentleman called Loa Anderson, his interest was based on the sides name being similar to that of his own. I supplied a lot of facts for him and later found out that he had used them for work and produced a TV programme on the club and the League. He was head of Sport at Swedish Television. I was invited over for the Sweden v Scotland match, but didn't take up his offer. Shortly afterwards he was transferred to head of Children's TV at the same station. We kept in touch until I moved back south. In fact when I moved I suddenly lost a lot of so called friends, and became aware of "hangers on", this feeling I keep with me and although retain a lot of famous friends, tend to keep them at arms length in case I am viewed as a so called "hanger on!" I wonder if Loa is still at Channel One in Sweden? One person I kept in touch with until his death recently was the old Ealing comedy actor Cardew Robinson. A self confessed Alloa nut. I always used to send him programmes to his Twickenham flat and receive interesting and humorous letters by return. He asked if I could write a book on the history of the club. I thought it was a good idea, but was asked not to by a gentleman called George Mathieson. He was an Alloa old boy. Been with the club since the year dot, was Secretary when they were promoted in 1939 etc. and a very respected person around Recreation Park. He wanted to write a book and didn't want me stealing his glory, so I backed off. George never got round to writing and died a few years ago. With the passing of each generation goes a lot of memories lost forever, I wish he had written about his experiences!

Following an unsuccessful 2 - 1 defeat at Montrose, I commented to one of the directors that the successful visit to Hampden should be repeated providing a Queens Park official would allow us to bring a couple of junior supporters on a tour. It was agreed and arranged "Providing I looked after the brats",
as Mr J.M.Keddie described the thought of having kids on the team

bus. The team were now second in the league mid way through September. Comments of we will get nose bleeds existing at this height were thrown around the ground by nervous supporters. Alex responded by organising another close door friendly to look at some new talent. This time the opposition were Dunipace United one of the most senior amateur sides around, I duly turned out to make up the numbers and to rest some of the first team squad. We drew 2 - 2 with my playing on the right wing and getting no where near the goal. Unknown to me at the time Alex was already looking for a replacement for Stan Drummond and the Dunipace keeper, Michael McGowan was shortly to join our squad.

October arrived and the Supporters Club picked two junior Supporter's names from a hat : Paul Martin and Willie Bell. Once they got onto the bus they were my responsibility. Having conquered the elder statesmen on the Alloa Board, I was about to find worse at Hampden. On arriving at the ground the doorman at the main Pavilion Door refused to allow the junior supporters access to the building despite having agreed it with the club. He was under instruction not to let anyone other that players into the dressing room. Guests to the board room. We proceeded to the boardroom only to be denied admittance as the guests were not wearing ties. A verbal jobsworth battle ensued until Pat Lawlor told one of the Queens Park directors what was going on and we were promptly let into the dressing rooms. Not that the kids remained there long, they ran out of the white tiled room into the corridor and onto the pitch. Hampden seems much bigger from the pitch than it does from the Directors Box! I used the mistakes made by Queens Park officials to my advantage and made the guests feel very important to make up for the embarrassment caused. They were formally introduced to both teams prior to kick off as if they were royalty. The looks on their faces was thanks enough. Both teams drew 1 - 1 and everyone went away happy after the event. I considered the Alloa Directors the lesser of two evils after that visit and started to work with them from that day on.

The month finished with Alloa flying high at the top of the league, despite a shock exit from the Stirlingshire Cup away to Stenhousemuir. I started to use my library records to do a series of articles on past famous players such as John White of Tottenham Hotspur who was killed on the golf course by a bolt of lightning. The feed back proved positive so I expanded it to cover the Promotion seasons. This was the start of problems with the printers. Having taken over printing for Albion Rovers as well they were starting to rush the printing and not check for errors. Mistakes were appearing in the programme. Their days as suppliers to the club were now numbered!

November quickly brought about a case of deja vous at Shawfield Stadium. I was refused entry by Clyde officials despite wearing club uniform and stepping from the bus. Only intervention by Alex Totten resolved the matter. This happened again when we revisited the stadium on 11th April, but then I was talking to supporters prior to entering the dressing room and was probably mistaken for a supporter. I was allowed in on production of my Players Pass. The club were not all bad as I returned there on a scouting mission during 1994 - 95 season at their new stadium in Cumbernauld. The Manager Alex Smith recognised me from when he was Stirling Manager and we watched the reserve match from the sponsors lounge.

Alloa won 3 - 0, and having succumbed to pressure from myself Arthur Montford from Scottish Television came along to watch. Scottish TV was all Celtic & Rangers with spluttering of the rest of the Premier League, outside of the division no coverage was given, so I complained several times. Arthur liked what he saw and Alloa were featured beating Queens Park 5 - 2 on 29th November. Before anyone could get excited though, it lasted 30 seconds as the goals were shown only. Still it was a start! Now Sky are around coverage is a little better, but the lower divisions are still ignored. TV viewers are missing out on some decent football!

4th November brought a welcome surprise Celtic agreed to supply the opposition for another close door friendly. I got the last 10 minutes in midfield as the game finished 2 - 2. I was able to renew acquaintances with Paul McStay and John Sludden who were on the Celtic side that evening. No really famous stars were on show as we were doing the Bhouys a favour by playing them to let them try out some new trialists.

The club faltered slightly by going down 4 - 0 at home to Montrose and lost the leadership of the division when they lost 3 - 1 to Albion Rovers at the dilapidated Cliftonville Stadium. One of my least favourite grounds!, however with the STV cameras present and following a kick by Alex the 5 - 2 victory over Queens Park restored them to the top. The following week was a trip to Brechin the pressure was on and although they drew 1 - 1 they became separated from the chasing pack and clear leaders of the division. The celebrations went over the top on the long bus trip home. We all stopped off for a meal and light refreshment to break up the journey. The result was Lex Shields and a couple of directors being the worse for drink. Lexy however ended up bouncing from seat to seat totally out of his head. He was always an extrovert so everyone saw the light hearted side of things and he was not fined by the club.

Despite an early exit at the hands of our bogey side Stenhousemuir in the 1st Round of the Scottish Cup things went from strength to strength and the club went 8 points clear at the top. The critics and TV pundits said we were absolute certainties for promotion.

Yet they blew it! And did so in a big way. Alex was screaming and shouting quoting Bill Shankley and what he was taught whilst at Liverpool, but it didn't do any good. From top of the table for most of the season they lost 2 - 1 at Hampden at the end of February. They achieved two draws the rest of the season, lost 1st place at the end of March and following two humiliating defeats 1 - 5 at home to Queen of the South, then 4 - 1 away to Forfar the club finished in 6th place. The ecstatic supporters lost confidence and a "told you so" crept around the ground.

I took my usual weeks holiday back to Chalfont to coincide with my birthday as a result of a letter I had received from Roy Castle of Record Breakers fame. Some of my colleagues at other clubs including T. Grant Cullen at Albion Rovers and Allan Grieve at Stirling had done some research and found I was the youngest Programme Editor in existence. This was later confirmed and the Press went to town over the event. The Alloa Advertiser carried an article, followed by the Bucks Free Press and several other Newspapers around my home town. Roy lived in Gerrards Cross the next village to Chalfont and he let slip to a journalist about my claim. David Puttnam asked me down to Chalfont's game with Redhill and hold a press conference. I shyed away from the publicity a little as I try not to let success go to my head! After Chalfont lost 4 - 0 which kind of reminded me of events back home, I met up with the journalist and did the usual interview, photos etc., Not the most flattering of photos appeared but I was happy to see that they were taking an interest in me. However, the story has a sting in the tail. Whilst I hold the record it will never be published as to include the event will lead to every other event needing to be recorded. The Guinness Book of Records would then double in size and so they made a decision not to publish any record to do with Sports Ages. At least that was the story I heard from Roy!

Just prior to the trip Alan finally got round to tying the knot with Karen, he was having a good season again and finished up top goalscorer that season with 15 goals.

Towards the end of the season I realised that come August Alloa would be playing their 60th season in the Scottish League. The Directors had no intention of celebrating and George Mathieson was still insistent about not doing a book. I decided to produce a handbook. The Directors mumbled something along the lines of finance, so I had to produce a budget and cash flow forecast. After meeting with the Printers in Coatbridge and being promised production within two weeks of receiving it. I worked out how much advertising space was needed and how many sales would be gained. The result however, was a disaster as a result of the printers letting the club down not for the first time.

Above: Myself; Doug Lawrie; Trevor Smith and John Cousin doing charity work for the local mentally handicapped school.
Below: 1st Day back Training with Alloa (number 10)

I spent three months putting together a 64 page book and gained finance through advertisers to pay for 3/4 of the production costs. Sales would only have to be about 50 to break even. I pre-sold the book to most Programme Editors in the lower two divisions, then the printers took on too much work and couldn't complete the task on time. Rather than take on temporary employees to assist they struggled on and excuse followed excuse and no handbook. It arrived shortly after Christmas when all the enthusiasm had gone. We had lost the start of season interest as well as the possibilities of gaining sales as Christmas presents. The printers ceased to print the programme for the club as soon as a suitable alternative was found.

However, personal drama was unfolding at home. United Glass had had a major internal reorganisation and my dad had been made redundant. After 6 months he had an opportunity to work in the Falklands, given what happened there about 12 months later I think it was a blessing we decided not to move. Possibilities arose in Mexborough and then Warrington. It soon became apparent that a move was inevitable and I would not be at Alloa FC at the end of 1981!

Below: Ian Smith posing when I called for a photo shoot for the handbook.

Chapter 5
All Change

In June it was confirmed that dad had found a new job with Ideal Toys in Wokingham, Berks. So a move was definite. I hurried along the handbook and completed it by the middle of July after meeting up with Alan Hansen and arranging for him to write an article for the book. Similar articles were also supplied by the Scottish League and Football Association, as well as Bob Wilson and Archie McPherson. A competition was run to design the cover which was won by John Anderson, a young supporter from Tullibody. Based on some rejected designs I designed the programme cover for my last season at the Rec.'s. The finished design took top honours at the end of season annual awards. The cover was voted top design for the Scottish League 1981 - 82 season. An accolade which although I achieved the honour the bulk of the glory shone on my successor who had taken over the programme from me and maintained the design 100 %.

That was the handbook put to bed, now a replacement for myself had to be found. I was not happy at the thought of leaving the club, but as I still lived at home and had no employment that would warrant a mortgage I had to go with my family. George Ormiston was very supportive, but couldn't find a replacement. So I pressed on editing the programme for as long as possible. Delays followed at the printers with the start of the season approaching. If the handbook non arrival wasn't bad enough. Issue one of the programme didn't arrive at the ground till half time so most of the Falkirk fans went away very unhappy at not being able to obtain a programme. By now I was getting the estimates reasonable accurate for production numbers which ranged from 250 to 1, 000 depending on the match. Normally I would be left with about 50 copies left so achieving the best possible profit margins for the Directors.

The 1st issue didn't contain the Manager's notes. For which Alex Totten stormed into the dressing room demanding to know why I

hadn't written any notes. My response was
"Because I'm not the manager",
he replied
"you are in my absence as far as the programme is concerned!"
At which point I suggested I gave the team talk, not the best thing to do when Alex is in a temper. He promptly attempted to dunk me in the showers fully clothed. Revenge was achieved by him at training the following week when he ordered Penalty Kick practice with me in goal. He got the entire squad to shoot at once. Point taken Alex!

The season started with a 4 - 1 friendly thrashing of Tulliallan Thistle and a 3 - 3 draw with Rangers. I turned out for the Tulliallan match and played in defence. I was rapidly becoming a utility player. The season really started where it had left off up in Forfar, but this time in the League cup, now organised into sections. As if to say nothing changes the score was the same. Losing 4 - 1 was probably the worst thing we could have done. In hindsight whereas we were expected to go up the previous year and failed miserably. Now we were being tipped to finish bottom of the league. Alex duly responded by ensuring the team won honours and went up in style.

For the Forfar game Tony Incenzo was back up and staying with my parents, so I quickly arranged for him to travel to the game on the team bus. We were Stirling Albion's guests for their friendly with Kilmarnock. Allan Grieve even managed to give us a tour of the ground, after completing his Programme duties. Even my dad came along to one of his rare matches. Tony then completed his visit with a tour round the Rec.'s and taking in the cup game with Falkirk which was a creditable 1 - 1 draw.

My search for a replacement Editor was at an end or so I thought. George Lloyd who was also on the supporters club committee agreed to take over the reigns, then changed his mind a week before I moved as he considered he had not enough time to spend writing it. As I was still writing I was not too put out, but I had to act fast.

My last game was against Stirling in the cup. The papers used it to promote my defecting to the Auld Enemy as they refer to England.

The photo was the worst I have ever seen of me, but it highlighted my case and my old school friend David Cooper agreed to take over, but only after a few more games as he had studies to complete. This meant all my facts and figures were left with him and I was faced with writing several more programmes from England without any information. Quite a challenge, only let down again by the printers, who had now taken over production of Airdrie's programmes as well. The Stirling programme I finally won my long battle to increase the programme to 16 pages and keep the price at 15p. Allan Grieve commented that it was the best programme he had seen in Scotland that year. Being August I told myself he hadn't seen many programmes yet, but fine praise from a competitor. August was quite a time for change. My old mate Alex Rae had accepted the manager's job at Forfar, Joe Baker, the former Arsenal and Scotland player who had played alongside me at the All Star match was put in charge of Albion Rovers, Terry Christie had taken over at Meadowbank Thistle, Neil Hood was sacked by Stranraer. Tony Ford had taken over from Bobby Moncur at Hearts and Dumbarton had just sacked Sean Fallon and replaced him with Billy Lamont. All within the space of a few weeks.

The day after the Stirling match Alex Totten phoned me at home to wish me luck and hoped I would come back and visit, I did later in the season.

Monday arrived and we said our fair wells and headed down South, I had to unpack then edit a programme for that Saturdays game with Forfar in the cup and post it to the printers to arrive by Wednesday. Somehow I did it! The programme contained Feature articles that I had put together on the English game, I don't know how it was received but the only other alternative was no programme, so I hope it was appreciated. The following week was the start of the league programme with Forfar the visitors again. The printers again let me down by not including a Manager's message. Their excuse was Alex hadn't posted it to them in time. I let George Ormiston take over the negotiations and rid myself of these printers. By the time the handbook had finally arrived in Mid January a replacement printer had been found in Tillicoultry. The handbook was praised nationally as the best ever produced by any club in Scotland. My first book in print and I was a success! As a result of the time factor of publication dates described earlier not as many copies were sold as was hoped. I believe copies are still for sale in the club shop if anyone is interested.

I can't help but wonder what would have happened to my career in Scotland had my dad not been made redundant and we had remained in Alloa. Sadly the answer to that question will never be known!

Above: Handover of the prize to John Anderson for his winning handbook design.
Below: Trials for Reading, my time with them was to be short!

Below: Handover time. The winning handbook and programme, with David Cooper and myself.

Now residing in Wokingham I couldn't just sit around I needed to join a club. Tim McWilliam at Wokingham Town invited me to join them which I readily accepted. However, this was on a non paid basis so whilst assisting with the programme production I looked around.

First stop was Elm Park and Reading FC. I was invited for a trail but not a lot happened after that. I obviously didn't fit into their plans. I was asked to write for the club programme, however, my first article was published and never sent to me. Tim at Wokingham found a copy of the programme v Brentford and I could understand why it had been kept from me. 90% of it had been changed to the extent it portrayed the exact opposite and as it was based on my happy times with Alloa, it now read that I was highly critical of the club and hated it. Not to mention the lies. I had a row with Andrew Album at the club and walked out. A local press release linked me with Aldershot Town, but I never went near the club so I don't know were that came from.

David Puttnam approached me to join Chalfont. How could I not work for MY club? Well they were about an hours drive from Wokingham and given my other commitments was unable to commit to what David wanted. I agreed to supply some free articles for the programme so continuing the family line. At Christmas David moved to Fleet and took over at Fleet Town. I was again approached but had to turn it down for the same reasons. I then joined a company called Duplex Litho, who had the contract to supply printed programme inserts for numerous clubs including: Altrincham; AFC Bournemouth; Bristol Rovers; Bury; Boston Utd; Bideford Town; Charlton Athletic; Chester; Colchester Utd; Crewe Alexandra; Corby Town; Exeter City; Molesley; Halifax Town; Hungerford Town; Kettering Town; Kidderminster Harriers; Northampton Town; Plymouth Argyle; Reading; Shrewsbury; Stockport County and Torquay Utd. Portsmouth's programme was printed by Duplex although no insert was used. A fee was agree of a minimum of £5 per article with a few complimentary programmes thrown in was agreed and I set about producing articles for them. Normally between one and three per issue. It was a nice little earner for me when they paid up. I should have foreseen a problem for although all my articles went to print I only received payment for some and on 26th February 1982 the company called in the receivers and were wound up I was left owed over £70 for unpaid articles.

Having my articles appear in Charlton's programmes was a dream come true, I retain all their programmes from that season in my collection. Halifax Town then contacted me. Tony Thwaites, the Commercial Manager and Programme Editor I had met a few years earlier when Alloa visited the Shay for a pre season friendly. He had read the articles and put two and two together. The club as today was in dire financial straits and needed support. Tony is one of those people who you can not fail to dislike and has a wonderful personality so I was only too happy to join him and help out. My reward was shares in the club which I hold to this day. I was attached to the club for several seasons, and met up with Tony whenever I could including at a Cup match at Tottenham which he missed due to other commitments, but allowed me his officials pass to watch the game in style. I regained contact with the club towards the end of 1994 - 95 season when they were about to go bust. I met up with Elaine Jowett prior to their last ever away match at Bromsgrove Rovers in the Conference on 22nd April and made a few suggestions that helped. The manager John Bird duly presented me with a signed ball after the game thanking me publicly for my support. The club was saved not totally as a result of my suggestions but I would like to think it helped. I met up with Elaine in her offices down the road from the Shay prior to the start of 1995 - 96 season and viewed the situation for myself. The club are struggling from one day to the next like many others a sorry situation which would only get better if the locals all supported the club instead of travelling to see Leeds United or dare I say it Manchester United play. A situation which is so familiar at all local lower league clubs. Elaine provided me with a framed signed shirt with an engraved label "Presented to Stuart Latham in Recognition of Help Given 1995". I was really taken aback by the kindness and friendliness of the club. The shirt is still hanging in my dining room along with a few other souvenirs I have collected from this wonderful sport. I will always have a soft spot for Halifax Town even if my shares are technically worthless I maintain my £1 a week in their lottery as well as in Alloa's I have never won in either though, funny that!

Meanwhile back at Finchampstead Road, Wokingham...:

Their Manager Roy Merryweather greeted me with open arms. He is very much a larger than life character and non league's equivalent to Barry Fry. I very quickly formed a strong friendship which continues to this day. Initially he was very interested in making comparisons with his club to that of a Scottish League club and was surprised to find that their was not much difference especially in the now Divisions Two and Three. Whilst committed to write articles for Duplex I relaxed at the club and quickly settled in helping at their twice a week Whippet racing evenings at the ground. I was assigned to assist in the editing of the programme whilst signing on for the club. I was in the Youth and Reserve teams alongside Roy's son Kevin and a good friend of mine Greg Tomlin. It was my responsibility to write match reports for the programme on the two teams which takes on a different concept when you are on the pitch taking part. If you are fouled by the opposition who then swears at you, you do not get the note book out and ask him how he spells it! The Isthmian League had a newspaper and it wasn't long before their journalist was hot on my heals. I was promptly interviewed and an article appeared in the paper. The article went a bit over the top announcing the club were heading for success having just signed me and Will Dixon the former Swindon, Reading and Aldershot player, but knowing journalists who am I to complain? Playing was through pure competition, being a utility player stood me in good stead. The goalkeeping door was firmly shut in my face as the club had several excellent young keepers in Steve Aldham and Trevor Hemmings. Steve and I sponsored each other in the programmes and although we both left the club as players met up on occasions several times after that when he was at Chertsey and I was with Cobham. Trevor and I both knew each other from my experience at Reading. We trained together there now found each other as team mates a few miles down the road. Of the rest of the squad, Phil Alexander went on to play for Norwich then onto fame as Commercial manager at Swindon and now Crystal Palace, although his most famous part was as kicker for the London Monarchs in the World American Football League a few years ago. Kirk Corbin went onto play for Cambridge United. Steve Butler to Watford and Maidstone, He is now enjoying success with Gillingham.

The Mitchell brothers gave up football and took up Ice Hockey playing for the Swindon Wildcats and the Bracknell Bees. Terry Brown succeeded on the non league Circuit and is currently the Manager of Conference side Hayes Town. Bradley Pratt moved around the local clubs and featured on BBC's Match of the Day programme when his clubs got through to the first round proper of the FA Cup.

Dad's company being based in the town sponsored the under 10's league which the club had a side in so all in all we all tried to help the club. The programme finished 5th in the annual Wirral Programme Club awards which was of great comfort given that 470 clubs in the non league circuit submitted issues. Roy achieved two Managers of the Month awards in October and January no less than he deserved. And the first team went up as champions of the Berger Isthmian League Division One. Both my clubs that year had won promotion. I had reason to feel proud! As to my performances at the club, well I had a problem. My favoured position was down the right wing and I was clashing with Clive Gale whose father Chas was Manager of the side. He favoured his son rather than me, favouritism, possibly but I didn't stand a chance. I played a total of 13 games for the club the whole season, before having an argument with Chas and finding myself on a loan period to Bracknell Town who played in the Spartan League.

I took some time away from Wokingham and took up Tony Incenzo's offer at QPR. I was unable to see the first professional game on astro turf as his Mother wanted to go, understandable as it was her season ticket. I made the second match when they beat Blackburn Rovers 2 - 0 on 3rd October.

Chris, dad and I got to Highbury to see Arsenal play Liverpool in the 4th Round of the League cup on 1st December. I had mixed feelings as my family were supporting Arsenal and my friend Alan Hansen was playing for the opposition. The best result all round occurred as a stalemate was reached 0 - 0. Liverpool won the replay 3 - 0 but I was not present to suffer.

April arrived and as I could not have a journey down south I went North and stayed with David Cooper for a week. I visited the Rec.'s and saw them beat Meadowbank 2 - 0 to virtually guarantee themselves promotion. The Annual Programme awards had just been made and the Alloa Advertiser were ready for the press call and obligatory photo session. The resulting photo appears on page 41.

The most embarrassing moment of the season occurred when we played Southampton Youth Team on 2nd November. I was on the Subs bench warming up when the crowd left the bar to watch the game. It was extremely wet conditions, I turned and fell on my face covering myself in mud. I got up to find team mate Paul Mitchell and half the crowd laughing at the spectacle. I sat on the bench throughout that game looking like a cocoon in the tracksuit and coveralls that were issued to me. I missed the following game and to my delight they lost 10 - 0. It didn't change Chas's mind on team selection so I knew I was on the way out. Chas didn't last long as Manager, if I had stuck it out who knows what would have happened!

Chapter 6
On the Move

Bracknell Town could not afford me so 1982 - 83 season saw me back at Finchampstead Road. The club had arranged several big friendlies. After defeating Stoke City 2 - 1, they played Oxford United on 9th August. To my surprise I was named as one of the substitutes. I got 20 minutes in the second half and hit the cross bar from a shot outside the box. Wokingham eventually won 1 - 0, but that was to prove to be my last match in their Amber and Black colours!. Bracknell Town called on my services once again for a 0 - 0 draw in a friendly with Marlow on 17th August. But they were not interested in signing me on. The Reserve Team Manager Tony Moody wanted me but the committee said no. Whilst they were thinking over their options I signed for Bracknell Spartans who played in the Premier League of the local Sunday League, sponsored by the local sports shop John Woods Sports. I was not the only Senior player on their books. I had five Hungerford Town players and Phil Henry the Goalkeeper from Bracknell Town to keep me company. I kept attending training at Bracknell Town under their Manager Steve McClurge on Tuesday evenings, to keep myself fit. However, Tony got fed up with his Directors attitude and demanded more power within the club. He was denied it and turned down an offer from Camberley Town whilst he sorted out Bracknell. He asked me to stay on as Programme Editor for the season, but as he had no authority within the club I said no as I had no commitments from the club. Tony Left and once I had won the Spartan League Challenge Trophy and Spartan League I left to join Maidenhead United.

By now I was working in retail and Saturdays were work days unless I had an understanding Manager. However, if I was selected I got the afternoon off at the expense of my day off during the week, so it worked very well. I was Assistant Manager at the Ripolin Paint Shop in Maidenhead so going to United was a good step. Their ground was only 10 minutes walk from the Nicholson's Walk Shopping Precinct so I accepted the offer to join them. Jon Swan the Programme Editor quickly realised he was on to a winner and before too long I found myself contributing to articles in the programme.

Chas's wife Ann contacted me on behalf of Roy to request my help in producing a News Letter called "Town Crier" which they hoped to circulate throughout the league. I accepted the call and contributed occasionally to the sheet which appeared in several clubs programmes including Harrow Borough's in 1984, when Town played there on 4th February 1984. I continued with my sponsorship of Steve Aldham and Bobby Saunders in the Wokingham Programme as a result.

I played on several occasions for Maidenhead United during the season, but found work commitments too much. I could make the second half or see the first half only but no more as I was under pressure from my Area Manager to be in the shop at the busiest period. This left evening matches only, so whilst I trained with Maidenhead the games I appeared in became few and far between.

Greg Tomlin helped organise a trip to Wembley to see England play West Germany on 13th October, as this was to be the first International match I had attended, I readily accepted his offer to come along. England lost 2 - 1. I got out and watched a few games, whilst keeping my association with Roy at Wokingham Town. Tony invited me back to Loftus Road to watch QPR beat Burnley 3 - 2 in a 2nd Division match. I had two trips to Aldershot to see them win 2 - 1 each time against Crewe and Hereford, even venturing up to Watford to see the Herts. Senior Cup Final where they beat Borehamwood 1 - 0. Not forgetting the return trip up north to see Alloa defeat Ayr United 3 - 0 in a first division game. This was definitely a season for change. Working in retail was to seriously hamper my playing career, but in the long run it probably helped keep me keen and enthusiastic about the sport. Maidenhead's programme production was continuous but the numbers issued were less than I had hoped for. I still miss issues in my collection of programmes containing my articles in as they sold out on the day. The friendly issue against Slough Town, being the most sort after. I received good feed back from Slough supporters and even Marlow fans who had made the short trip to see the game, but no copy was available. I had a good look round the club shop at Wexham Park when I visited on 4th April for a match where I was very much caught in the middle. The Berks. and Bucks. Cup Final this year had thrown Wokingham and Bracknell together, I knew and trained with both squads for the past two seasons so having loyalties to Roy, I suppose I was not too unhappy when they beat Bracknell 2 - 0. Some local TV cameras were present, which was most unusual as non league was uncharted territory for film crews! And so back to York Road. Maidenhead United had a strong squad and I was privileged to train with John Dempsey before he left the club towards the end of the season. His experience at Chelsea was passed on and I learnt quite a lot.

By now the articles were flowing fast as I was inundated with requests for work. If only they had paid well I would have been a rich man today.

First off the block were Brechin City of all clubs! They had set up a supporters club in Bury St Edmunds and I was asked to provide some information, which I did throughout the season. The result was one of the first fanzines ever produced. Tony Incenzo heard about it and also lent his support with his usual article on himself, talk about self publicity! He then followed this up with a book on his F.A.Vase exploits called Tansley to Wembley. Then the ego received a further boost when he joined Fisher Athletic at the Surrey Docks Stadium and edited the Pyramid magazine, which is a magazine for non league fans by non league fans. I contributed items for this monthly magazine from its 4th issue till its 44th. By then I had started to concentrate on other more important issues.

Then came the now firmly established Programme Monthly. I was there from the start in February 1981 and contributed on occasions for several seasons.

Tony introduced me to a band of football fanatics called the Continentals. They come from Holland and watch British matches and visit as many grounds as they can. I made several friends over their, including Ad Poot who is a lifelong Charlton Athletic supporter. Then Henk van der Sluis a devoted Leicester City Nut who was a school teacher near the Hook of Holland. Willem van Ekelenburg, Jan Buitenga and Johannes de Boer. This was a meeting at Wimbledon's training ground on 3rd April when the Dutch were challenged to a friendly by Wimbledon. The outcome was a resounding 13 - 4 victory for the Don's. Who said they couldn't score goals? This was a match that couldn't be viewed on Ceefax! By this time Tony had stayed at all the Continental's houses and seen matches at all the senior Dutch clubs so was losing interest in this band of supporters. Henk took me to one side and made a few comments about Tony not realising I knew him very well. This started an interest in Dutch Football which carried on for several years.

Chapter 7
Going Dutch

Of the Continentals their were several very influential people. Jan Hermen DE Bruijn as Chairman of the group was a professional journalist; Jan Buitenga, a Tax Inspector; Willem Van Ekelenburg a Dentist, who was always known as the oldest swinger in town. His favourite song and spent most of his spare time in England trying to find the Fred Wedlock record without success in music shops. Henk van der Sluis who as well as being a teacher was a qualified Water Polo referee. His English was excellent but his phases often let him down. He hated arriving at football grounds after kick off and was the centre of much amusement when being interviewed by the local press after a match as to his dislikes promptly replied
"Coming too late!".
At over 6 foot tall and weighing 20 stone he was easy to spot. And Eric van der Polder. His Dad was Holland's top Sports Journalist.

I was approached by Henk to visit Holland and see some games. Eric wanted me to visit him in Rotterdam and see his favourite side Feyenoord play. I accepted and 1983 - 84 season got off to a flying start.

After watching Wokingham lose an entertaining match 4 - 8 to Stoke City, I sat in the stand next to Lou Macari and mentioned Holland, he took an interest as he knew several players who had failed to make the grade in England succeed on the Continent and gave me a couple of contact names. Meanwhile Eric's dad Dick, who writes under the alias of Vrije Volk and used to play for Excelsior in the Dutch League had fixed me up with a couple of trials using his contacts, so Henk planned a rather hectic week for me.

On landing at Rotterdam Airport, I was briskly collected and driven up the road to a small ground and introduced to a young team in the Junior League (Holland's equivalent of Non League) called Kosakken Boys Club just outside Rotterdam. 3/4 of the ground was open park, but surrounded by tall trees. Yet they had a large solid high capacity stand. The League they played in was the equivalent to the Beazer Home League Premier Division. I nervously put on my strip un able to understand the coaches instructions, fortunately most of the team spoke English fairly well so I got by. However, the opposition was Sparta Rotterdam who fielded their entire first team squad. Playing at centre forward I could not get past their excellent defenders who tackled their way to victory. The result was a humiliating 10 - 0 defeat for Kos. I stayed at Henk's house in Naaldwijk for the duration and after making a mess of driving on the wrong side of the road and nearly driving against the flow of traffic at a cross roads on a dual carriageway, Henk offered to drive for the week.

The following day (5th) most of the group met up and asked me to contribute articles to their magazine and join in their prediction league. Probably the first Fantasy Football League in existence, this I readily accepted. Lunch in Rotterdam was at the local MacDonalds and I was pleased to note that Big Macs taste the same over their as they do over here. On the itinerary for me that night was the Feyenoord tournament. Liverpool were in town so we managed to find out where they were staying and popped up to see Alan Hansen. However, the person on reception refused to let me upstairs or speak to him over the phone. In the end he phoned up and pronounced my name in such a way that Alan did not recognise it and I left without seeing him. This was rather embarrassing and the look of disappointment on Eric's face said it all.

At the Stadium I witnessed my first experience of football hooliganism. The British had quite a reputation for hooliganism prior to their ban from European competition, but this event showed how much this country was made scapegoats. The Dutch fans had organised themselves perfectly, and planted their key men at both corners of the ground. Those in Feyenoord colours charged the Liverpool supporters, who retreated and ran to the corner of the ground where a lot of other Liverpool fans were standing. Only they were Feyenoord in disguise. The trap had worked and like Custers

Last Stand the Liverpool supporters were surrounded and out numbered. Serious fighting broke out and had it not been for the swift action of the police serious injuries would have been sustained. Fortunately for me I was watching from high up in the stand and well away from danger. The nearest I had come to trouble prior to this was at the Arsenal v Liverpool match, two seasons previously when both club's supporters charged each other in the Avenal Road. Chris promptly threw me into the nearest Garden to avoid being hit. Both sets of fans were letting off steam and probably because of the heavy police presence that evening nothing happened. Liverpool drew with Hamburg 0 - 0 but went out of the tournament 3 - 4 on penalties. Part of the stadium then emptied as the second match of the day started. Feyenoord going down 3 - 0 in front of their own fans to Standard Liege.

After the excitement of the previous day Henk had planned to go to Deventer to see that evenings match between his side Go Ahead Eagles and an Austrian side A K Grazier. Deventer is very similar to Arnham having the same bridge and towers. Arnham had changed since the second world war, whereas Deventer had remained the same. It was because of this that the town was used as the base to film the movie blockbuster. A Bridge Too Far. I found the day passed peacefully and discovered the ultimate in relaxation, and how clubs differ over there to those in England. Each club has its own bar/ Continental cafe, near the main entrance to the ground which is kept open. Supporters come and go as they please and sit on the terraces discussing the previous match and any team changes. The bar is open all day and on a hot day like it was that afternoon, I sat outside the Go Ahead Eagles club bottle of Amstel beer in one hand having a long chat with Henk and one of the players who was a very good friend of Henk's. A coloured Englishman with a lot of talent called Mike Small. He later came back home and played successfully in the Premiership with West Ham. Mike then took me on a tour of the ground and we watched them beat the Austrians 2 - 1 from the officials enclosure part of the stand.

Not content with a day off Henk was showing me round most of the league grounds on a tour of the country. Probably hoping I would sign for a side and remain in Holland. We ended up in Utrecht, mainly by my requesting it. Their stadium was impressive, but I wanted to see the tournament that was being staged their. Utrecht lost 6 - 5 after extra time to Belgian side Lockeren, but the game I wanted followed straight after. Nottingham Forest took on and beat a Romanian National X1 2 - 0.

I had the next day (8th) as a rest day of sorts a few more local league sides were visited whilst I prepared myself for my next trial.

DS'79 are a small Dutch 1st Division Club in Dordrecht. Their stadium "Krommedijk" is on par with the English 3rd Division and the standard is 1st or 2nd Division. Dick had arranged for me to guest for the side in their tournament. Unfortunately for me I was playing on day one and not on finals day. The first match came and I sat in the stand enjoying Everton run rings round Dutch league side Haarlem, eventually winning 3 - 1. Then it was my turn we played a rising Belgian side Mechalen who later went on to European glory. I had a bad game and didn't play as I had hoped. DS'79 won 2 - 1 and played Everton in the final. I unfortunately played no part in that game. My lasting memory of that day is on entering the ground. Outside their is a small lake and it was another hot day. This lake was full of fully clothed Everton supporters playing with blow up dolls oblivious to all the Dutch looking on in confusion.

The 10th arrived and I was nearing the end of my mammoth tour. I still had three games to go before flying home. The first was meeting up with another ex pat Rob MacDonald who promptly introduced his team mate Erwin Koeman to me. Rob played for Hull before moving to Groningen and was very popular over there. The resulting conversation persuaded me to come back again the following pre season and have a go. Both he and Erwin showed me round their Oosterparkstadion. By now all 1st Division grounds were starting to look the same. They were playing Nottingham Forest. Several Forest players stopped to talk to Rob and I as they made their way into the changing rooms, were another ex pat was waiting to talk to some of his old English friends. Len Cantello the former West Brom and Bolton player who was now making his fortune playing for SC Cambuur in the same league as Groningen. The Dutch side won 2 - 1. After the game Len invited me to look around the Cambuur stadium and facilities at Leeuwarden, which I took him up on his offer the following day prior to going to Zwolle, Go ahead Eagles rivals. They had also organised a tournament so we met up with Mike Small again who introduced me to Johnny Rep the former Dutch international who was now playing for PEC Zwolle'82. Both sides had been kept apart in the draw probably to ensure an exciting final. FC Twente beat Go Ahead 5 - 2 on penalties following a 1 - 1 draw. PEC Zwolle also drew with Heracles also of the Dutch League but went through 6 - 5 on penalties.

Then it was off home for a rest. Watching Bracknell draw with Brentford 0 -0 in a friendly 12 days after my flight home confirmed my enthusiasm to go back again next August.

Following Aldershot's loss at home to Hereford United 4 - 1 in the 4th Division and two further matches at Bracknell and Wokingham the month of August was rounded off in style with promotion at work. I was promoted to running my own Paint shop in Cobham Surrey. This meant that I had to leave Maidenhead United. I ventured down to Anvil Lane to watch a Combined Counties League match between Cobham and Frimley Green. The Combined Counties League is the feeder league for the Isthmian/ ICIS League so still good quality Being me I started talking to the crowd not that there was many and one thing led to another and I joined them. I was to remain with the Hammers until I got married in 1987 and moved to Swindon, making travelling too difficult.

Secretary Barrie Harlow offered me the position of Public Relations Officer and doing the match reports for the local press, plus a place on the committee. When I inquired about programmes I was duly told that they didn't issue them. Suddenly finding myself a big Cog in a very small wheel I decided to do something about it.

Starting from scratch isn't as easy as you might think especially when production costs have to be borne in mind and committees hate spending money unless it is warranted! The economics of the venture must be given careful consideration, especially in these days of stringent financial restrictions. How much will it cost to produce? Printer's quotes must be obtained and these costs evaluated against printing quality and services offered; i.e. how near to match days must the editorial material be in the printers hands? Could late changes be included? Is there any cost limit for inclusion of pictures? What increase in cost would result from including extra pages? After a suitable printer has been found, the advertisements must be found. Some clubs look to their programmes as a source of large income, but some try to balance their programme, giving maximum reading material and a minimum of adverts. - A minimum of adverts that is, that the advertisement revenue will cover any loss invoked during sales.

A prediction of sales over the season must be made, although until the programme actually goes on sale this is a matter for conjecture. It must be also considered that if the team has a lean season, crowds will be poor and sales will fall. On the basis of minimum sales the price can now be fixed, initially to cover - along with adverts revenue - the cost of production over the season. Anything over this could be considered a bonus initially, and would be the basis for further progress.

Normally at this stage, the advertising space is considered as page area; i.e. so many pounds per quarter, half, or full page etc. Then comes the hard graft, tramping round the local businesses trying to sell the advertising space. Initially it is easy as the first businessmen you visit are normally friends of the club or supporters, and most are only too happy to help. Thereafter, the task to interest the more indifferent businessmen to subscribing to an advert. This can often be difficult, as inevitably the conversation gets round to the team and one often ends up defending them against criticism. However, sooner or later the advertisement problem is settled and we sit back and wait for the advert copy to arrive.

Then comes the practical aspect of the reading material. Contact the Manager of the team and determine whether he will contribute regularly to the programme. Then interview the players and get their pen pics; if it can be arranged a photo session is useful, with individual player pictures and a team group photo a must. Then the feature articles must be written and it is a good thing if persons other than the Editor contribute regular articles.

Then the big day arrives - the first issue and you wait with baited breath to see how it looks and then ask people for constructive criticism.

Before it goes on sale, programme sellers must be recruited. On the first day we eagerly scrutinise the day's takings and there is joy or despondency over the sale of the programmes. At most games what is done with the surplus stocks? Are they sold in the club shop or traded with other clubs. All these matters must be looked into so I spend a few hours preparing a business plan for my first committee meeting. Come the meeting I patiently awaited my turn and brought out copies of my plan. At which point the Treasurer turned round and said "Can't afford it. Tell you what, you type it and well get it photo-copied!"

I returned to Chalfont to see them beat Marlow and go top of the Athenian League for the first time. A slight change had happened at the club and now Veronica Turner was the Social Secretary. She was keen to meet me as she had gone to school with my mother. I agreed to help out towards the end of the season providing it didn't clash with my other commitments.

A trip to Wembley to see England lose 1 - 0 to Denmark in the European Nations Cup was next on the agenda, before starting my programme production at Cobham. First stop was to Wokingham to see Roy and I agreed to supply articles and news items from the Combined Counties League in return for having free copies of their new newsletter for the programme. This was started off as an idea to rival Duplex's earlier efforts. The 4 page item lasted the season and I know of 4 clubs who took it on, but it died a death due to the lack of enthusiasm shown by other clubs. Next stop was Aldershot who totally rejected a few proposals I put to them, as they had just lost 3 - 2 to Notts County in the Milk Cup I probably caught them at an awkward moment, and they were unprepared to discuss printing options. The end result was back to the photocopier.

Issue number one was for the FA Vase match with Erith & Belvedere. A 12 page edition was produced which immediately met with praise from the committee. Historically when the club issued a programme it was normally 4 or 8 pages. Straight away I had made an impression and decided to build on it. The squad had an experienced player in Ray Coombes who had played at Wembley a few seasons previously when Bishops Stortford reached the FA Trophy Final, plus a rising star in Keith Baker. He became a regular in the Farnborough Conference side a few seasons later and retained his place in their team for quite a few years. I kept the league programmes at 8 pages whilst I established myself. Having signed on as a player I was mostly with the reserve team because of work commitments not guaranteeing my availability. So I made a few players happy by issuing for reserve matches as well. The morale factor amongst the teams were raised and from sitting bottom of the league a string of results were put together and they finished in a respectable position.

I returned to Maidenhead and collected some article copies I had left with the club just in case I ran out of ideas and ended up stopping to watch a cup match. Reading had brought forward their game with Crewe to a Friday night, so I went along to see Martin Hicks play for Readings 1st Team. He is still with them today! I bumped into Maurice Evans and found all the troubles from two seasons ago had been put behind them and now forgotten about. Having got the weekend off I left Bob Freeland in charge of programme distribution at the club and headed for Highbury to see the Gunners lose 1 - 0 to Coventry City.

David Coles, the Aldershot goalkeeper was once on Cobham's books and I met him on my last trip to the club. He invited me over for a testimonial match. The other goalkeeper Glen Johnson was retiring and Arsenal were to supply the opposition. I jumped at the chance 6 years late but I got to see the fixture I wanted! A creditable 3 - 3 draw was achieved. David mentioned Reg Madgewick and asked if he was still at the club. I said yes he was and still on the committee at 74 having given 30 years service to the club. I was then promised if I ever decide to honour him to let David know as he would like to show his appreciation. I kept that in mind.

David Puttnam then phoned me out of the blue. Fleet were having a lot of problems and needed a couple of good results quickly, "What did I know about Chertsey?"
My response was more sarcastic than helpful. When I realised he was on about the team I said no idea. Sô was asked if I could have a look at them and report back. So my first scouting mission had begun. Finding the ground was difficult and it was cold. This brought back memories of my trip to Brechin City on 6th December 1980. We had a new driver who got lost in the town that was so small it only had a population of about 6, 000. We spent an hour trying to locate Glebe Park, when we did find it a prevailing wind started a blizzard and the game was played under several inches of snow. As Chertsey was only a few miles from Cobham I braved the cold and eventually found the ground hidden. They lost to Redhill but put on a worthy display. The following week I went over to Fleet and told David the news. It didn't help as Chertsey won the match 1 - 0.

Several of my friends are loyal Chelsea fans and for several seasons I had rejected offers of going to Stamford Bridge. A mid week Milk Cup game with West Bromwich Albion coincided with my day off and I was dragged along instead of going football training. Not a lot was said and I ended up playing for the reserves at Fleet and we won 2 - 1 following some inside information I knew on which of their players were worth marking. David saw the funny side eventually.

With the arrival of the programme insert from Wokingham, I stepped up a gear and persuaded some of the advertisers that if they paid a little more then their adverts would appear on properly printed quality glossy pages. Everyone agreed as they current photocopies were passable. The extra revenue paid for 8 glossy pages to be produced, with my 8 pages of photocopy now advert free and allowing more space for articles. Wokingham Town then stepped in were Aldershot had refused to co-operate and Roy and I designed the new look programme. The local photographer wanted a gallery area to show off some of his work, The clubhouse was then made available with certain wall space permanently available to the owner Mr Strange. He was happy with the arrangement and promptly provided the teams with two sets of kit with his Company name emblazoned across the front. Team photos were then taken and both parties enjoyed a happy sponsorship period over the next three years with further income coming in from an Advertisement board and sponsorship money. At the end of the contract Mr Strange went one further and sponsored the entire Combined Counties League. The league is now sponsored by Dan Air I believe!

December proved to be particularly hectic. Traditionally a slow period for decorating shops, I used the time to my advantage. Mr Area Manager Jim Purkis started to show a little confusion as to why I never took a lunch break on Saturdays but disappeared for several hours on a Saturday afternoon only to return to cash up and phone the week's sales figures in. I had excellent staff who accepted my delegation without question and gave them time off when needed being the soft touch I am so everyone was happy. Jim made a few mutterings so having my old team mate from Wokingham Darren Barnard join Chelsea was a blessing in disguise! Jim supported Chelsea so Darren got an autographed ball for Jim. He never questioned my actions again.

Tony Thwaites arranged to meet me at Elm Park to see Halifax go down 1 - 0 to the by now high flying Reading. Several other matches went by without incident and I was now being overlooked in the reserve team. Christmas Eve arrived and I closed up the shop to venture down to the club. Tony Incenzo had by now completed all the Isthmian and Athenian League clubs and decided to start on our league, so I showed him round the facilities and we saw the first team lose to our neighbours Virginia Water 2 - 1.

I was asked to assist with unlocking the clubhouse and looking after the officials for the game on 27th with British Aerospace. Fortunately the kick off had been brought forward to 11am as I had already made other commitments. Cobham were played off the park and lost 3 - 0, I hardly stopped after the game as I did my first double of the season quickly rushing off to Elm Park where I had arranged to meet Tony Brown whom I had met through Duplex Litho in 1981 when he played in defence for Torquay United. A creditable 2 - 2 draw was achieved by the Gulls and it was to be the start of a long relationship with the Devon club which continues to this day.

Ash United under Dawn Reynolds had been producing one of the best programmes in non league levels for a few years now, their dominance was now under threat and Dawn and I often exchanged views and had a goodwilled personal battle for league supremacy. She charged nearly twice as much for her edition, but the funds allowed for better presentation. She was to win the battle with the Annual Wirral Programme Awards that year but not the war! The Gloss Programme covers arrived about Christmas and I leapt into action

Tony Incenzo found his way to Bracknell Town for their Berks. and Bucks tie with the mighty Wycombe Wanderers. It was the first time I got to meet Mike Keen and found him to be a very pleasant man. He said he hadn't seen my dad in years so we arranged to meet up in March when Wokingham entertained Wycombe in the Isthmian Premier League. This was to be dad's annual outing to a match. He had now decided to concentrate on his handicap. As he had just become a member at the exclusive Badgemore Park Golf Club in Henley he had to justify the expense and continues to play every week no matter what the weather. I met up with some of the press from the Bracknell News. The sight of journalists and the possibility of free publicity meant Tony was hovering trying to have an interview. It was to be a busy evening having just collected the programme covers from Roy, I was then asked to deliver that evenings programme to

Bracknell as Wokingham were now producing Bracknell's programme. Heavily overloaded I arrived at Larges Lane to find the press wanting copies and trying to find out the team. It was his first match covering a game in Bracknell, so I assisted. Luckily half the team were my team mates from the Bracknell Spartans Sunday League side so identifying them was not a problem. Chas Gale turned up for the match. He had now left Wokingham to become Assistant Manager of Camberley Town. His interest was as a former Wycombe player for 12 years. Pop Star Rick Wakeman had just taken over as Chairman at Camberley and hopes were high following their relegation to the Athenian league.

I did a triple issue programme over the Christmas period which was adjudged to be the best issue by a Combined Counties side that season. My name was starting to reach League clubs again and people were taking notice.

Cobham is in the middle of the stockbroker belt and claim to have more famous people living in the area than us lesser mortals. My shop was the only shop were most residents popped in for coffee whilst doing their weekly shop in Bejams and Tesco a few feet away from my unit. This started by accident. Dick Cornish was the local community Policeman. His son Mark played for Cobham and he popped in to introduce his young colleague who was to be taking over from him. I made them both a cup of tea as Sally James came in with her children. Even though it was several years since she finished working on Tiswas with Chris Tarrant (another native of the area) she was still as lovely as ever and I used to enjoy her popping in every now and then for a chat. She passed a few comments about my making this a tea shop. She then had a cup of coffee and then mostly during the week word got round and I found myself very popular with the locals. The shop did rather well out of it as well!

Reg decided over Christmas that at 74 he was going to stand down from the club committee at the end of the season, so as he was still a taxi driver in London used a committee meeting whilst he was working to introduce the idea of a testimonial match for him. The issue was agreed unanimously. A select side were to play an All Stars match at the end of the season. As I had suggested it I was voted the person best suited to organise it. Having made a lot of celebrities my friends getting a team together should be no problem. Wrong! Football is poorly supported in the area and not that many people wanted to help. Both Sally and Mollie Sugden showed no interest. Trevor Bannister had shunned publicity since his days on Are You Being Served and seemed on the verge of a nervous breakdown. Eric Sykes was busy playing Golf over at St Georges in Weybridge and was going very deaf and didn't want to make a public appearance. So I turned to footballers. Bobby Moore had just left his wife to move into a house with a pretty Air Stewardess in the Portsmouth Road and was extremely reluctant to show is face in public at that time so politely refused me. He later married the Stewardess and I was to see him again before un untimely death. He had time for not only myself but others as well and will be sorely missed! Geoff Hurst turned me down flat and my last vision of him was as I chased him down the High Street begging him to reconsider. So to Plan "B"!

The Club Treasurer Andy Dunkerley was also a qualified accountant and in January after looking into the books allowed me a budget to have a programme professionally printed for Reg's match. Being an ex Rochdale player he was used to "quality!" and wanted to see Reg go out in Style. Roy promptly agreed to offer Wokingham's printing facilities at cost which was an appreciated gesture. I would have no problems filling a programme.

63

Below: Cobham F.C.

My friends in the Metropolitan Police invited me over to Imber Court for a friendly against Denmark's under 21 side. The Danes won 5 - 1 and I witnessed the dirtiest match ever. Quite a shock considering they were policemen! I was then reinstated to the reserve team who promptly celebrated the fact (Well I can dream!) by beating Westfield 1 - 0 in a cup competition. A trip to Highbury to see Graham Rix score in an uneventful 1 - 1 draw with Aston Villa and an invitation back to Fleet by David passed and then a surprise! I was being noticed. Robert Wilson a young Fulham defender who lived near me in Winnersh had just got married and had nearly died as a result of carbon monoxide poisoning in his house contacted me and invited me to see Fulham's game with Newcastle. I readily accepted and saw Newcastle in their famous silver away strip draw 2 - 2 in what proved to be one of Kevin Keegan's last games as a player. Robert afterwards agreed to turn out for the testimonial match. Recruit Number one!

Looking for further ideas I saw Reading defeat Colchester 1 - 0 and met up with Maurice Evans who refused to let any of his players join in as they were going for promotion and didn't want to risk any injuries as I hadn't confirmed a date of the match. Mike Keen met up with my father at the Wokingham match and said he would ask his players but wouldn't promise anything. Roy then offered to send some of his names, including Roger Steer who had started his career at Chelsea; Terry Brown who I knew very well and Bobby Saunders with more if I needed them.

March was a particularly cold spell and the evening matches were struggling to beat the freezing pitches. As I sat watching Walton and Hersham beat Farnborough Town 3 - 0 frozen to the wooden seat in the stand I reminded my self that this was not the coldest spot in football. That honour goes to Arbroath whose stand is barely 20 yards from the North Sea. A friendly between Windsor and Eton and Arsenal loomed and after the Gunners 3 - 0 victory took my opportunity of approaching some of the Arsenal players. I was hurt to be rejected and not get even an offer of a signed ball for a raffle. Charlton Athletic to their credit did send a ball, having had a player from the club a few seasons earlier, and my allegiances were rapidly changing from mostly Arsenal to Charlton.

Chalfont St Peter were almost certain to be promoted in the final season of the Athenian League and I accepted the chance to revisit the ground for their match with Hoddesden. The point gained in the 3 - 3 draw guaranteed them a place in the new expanded Isthmian League the following year and I was again approached to join them. After pressure I joined them as Vice President for the forthcoming season. So establishing the family connection well and truly. A return to playing action for Cobham followed and the Surrey Senior League approached me to write a programme for their Cup Final which was to be staged at Cobham. I accepted. The league had contacts and the gesture went a long way.

Cobham played Yateley at home in the league and it was a return for some old school friends from Yateley Comprehensive, most notably the goalkeeper Stewart Adams I was unable to play due to work commitments but met up for a reunion after the match.

By now the season was drawing to a close. Mike Keen told me that his son Kevin would not be released by West Ham for the match and his players were not interested, but he would try to turn up on the day. Then a bit of luck. Mike Morris who was presenting on TVAM came into the shop to buy a tin of paint. Bribery took place, he couldn't play but agreed to turn up and lend his support in return for discount on his paint. A few hours later Michael Rodd came in and readily agreed to play. He decorated his house quite cheaply over the next few months! I found him one of the most down to earth of all my friends and am glad his TV career has taken off again on SKY. To kick off the match Ray Allen agreed to come along as long as he did not have to perform with Lord Charles. The squad was now taking shape. Next it was across Wokingham to see an old Goalkeeping friend, Phil Parkes. I had often helped do things for his wife Lavinnia and his children so I phoned him up. He was delighted to play. This did have a set back as he was shortly banned for drink driving and West Ham called him in to do extra training to teach him a lesson. Having a phone call from him on the day of the match was not the ideal preparation for the game, but he dropped over some signed West Ham items for the raffle and I realised it wasn't his fault that the other Hammers had put their foot down. His place was quickly filled by an old friend and later Best Man, Jason Parker, who was quite a talent when he tried on the pitch but languishing in Sunday League with FC Bracknell. David Coles came over from Aldershot and brought his player coach Ian Gillard with him. The match proved a great reunion for Ian.

Cobham's last league game brought a surprise as Eric Strange the owner of the club's sponsors had almost as warped a sense of humour as me arranged a publicity stunt. A happy hour was arranged in the bar before the match with Godalming and he timed to perfection a publicity stunt when the bar closed a few minutes before kick off when the supporters emerged from the bar a little worse from wear to find an elephant staring at them. As the elephant left the pitch it promptly lifted its tail and left a deposit in the home team dug out. I was glad not to be substitute that day!

The Annual programme awards were announced and the club achieved 51st nationally out of 625 entrants. We were let down by the photocopying. A 3rd Place in the league was the highest the club had ever achieved with their editions so the committee were more than happy. Dawn Reynolds won the league and got into the Top 10 with Ash United's edition. 1 - 0 to her!

I went to Highbury on my day off to get a ticket for the Arsenal v West Ham match on 7th May as Phil didn't have any spare complimentary ones and saw a Combination game. I missed kick off but a steward along with Jack Kelsey the former Arsenal and Wales goalkeeper accompanied me through the marble corridors past the bronze bust of Herbert Chapman to the dressing rooms and access to the stand to witness Raphael Meade destroy Swindon Town 8 - 0. On getting home I found that my friends Greg and Max had got a ticket for me to attend the Chelsea v Barnsley match the same day. Arsenal kicked off at 11 am and drew 3 - 3, Then I shot across London in time to meet the guys in a pub in the Kings Road, for a quick pint before watching Chelsea win 3 - 1 to gain promotion to the 1st Division.

The next two weeks were to be the busiest of the season. I met up with Simon Stainrod walking his dog with his wife Gillian along Anvil Lane and realised the solution to my problem was staring me in the face. Simon's house backed onto the ground. I told him about the match to which his response was

"What the old man, sure I'd love to let me know if you need any help and I'll ask the boys".

Perfect. Simon then brought down half of the Queens Park Rangers Squad including Gary Chivers who with Keith Stevens of Millwall and the Fulham scout that Robert had persuaded to turn up we had 1½ teams. The balance was then made up of Cobham players and we were ready for a match. Steve Finneston heard that Mike Fillery was playing so turned up on the day and was a welcome addition and knew everyone at the club as he was now playing in the same league with Hartley Wintney.

The match got under way with a flying start when "Cobham" scored in the first 30 seconds, the All Stars quickly made amends. Simon Stainrod kicked off by passing to myself who ran straight for goal, past two players and with only an advancing keeper to beat pasted it square to Simon to slot into an empty net. Ray Coombes restored "Cobham's" lead despite some dubious play from Roger Steer much to the dismay of his former Chelsea team mates. By half time the scores were level at 3 - 3 thanks to a goalmouth scrambled goal scored by yours truly. During Half Time Michael Rodd and I discussed an option which delighted the capacity crowd. Mike had offered to come off, but I told him to stay on and I replaced my self with Reg. The second half was again end to end and Reg amazed everyone by scoring a hat trick but it was not enough as the All Stars lost 8 - 7.

After the match we had the normal photo and autograph sessions. My mother came along to her 2nd match in a week but not to watch me play, but to see Ray Allen.

The players all joined in a party in the boardroom at the club's expense. I quickly learnt not to get into a drinking match with Mike Fillery who drank most of the bar dry. The bar had record takings and we ran out of scotch much to the dismay of Ray Allen who drank nothing else. It later came to light that the barman was a confirmed alcoholic and had drunk the whisky himself. He was dismissed from the club.

Roy and some colleagues from Wokingham Town and Chalfont St Peter turned up to lend their support which was a nice touch as did a mystery person from Tottenham Hotspur. A successful day all round!

Chalfont blew the Athenian League championship in style by drawing their last match of the season. Only a win would have done. My mother accompanied me to the game but saw none of it preferring to spend the time in the clubhouse chatting to old school friends. The club afterwards received a photocopier from myself as part of a sponsorship package I had put together for them.

That was the end of the season, or so I thought. We had our end of season Dinner Dance where I was given an FA Cup Final ticket by the committee for hard work over the season from their allocation from the Football Association. By the end of the evening I had received a second ticket from one of the other players who didn't want to go unless he had two so he could take a friend. I had never been to an FA Cup Final and wasn't about to give up my ticket, so at the end of the Dance he gave it to me.

After sleeping what was left of the night in the shop I returned home and surprised my father still in bed when I got home and we both went to see Watford lose to Everton 2 - 0.

Chapter 8
Year Of The Cockerel

At the club's Annual General Meeting Roy Osborn, the club's Secretary resigned and I was left without access to a photocopier, this was addressed by the rest of the committee taking a bit each of the programme and photocopying it. I then reassembled it on a Saturday morning.

The close season saw me change jobs three times. I left the shop to join the Royal Air Force and be a Pilot Officer along with my former school friend David Cooper, however, as I had suffered from asthma as a child briefly I was quickly discarded again after joining. The Tottenham Contact then re emerged and requested my presence at White Hart Lane. What followed was a two hour interview with Peter Day who was looking for a new Commercial Manager. It was eventually decided that my experience was vast but not of the level required by the club and I was not offered the position. Peter did comment on how impressed he was with me and hoped we would meet again soon. We Did! A change then happened by chance. One of my paint reps called on me with his Area Manager and I moved into Sales for ICI selling Dulux Paint into the DIY sheds.

On the advice of Peter Day who advised me to get some football qualifications, I contacted my Sunday League Referee Association Officials, an amenable Policeman named Peter Bentley and Nevil Batt. They were more than happy to put me through a Referees' Course and so I became a Class Three registered referee with the Berks. & Bucks Football Association and joined the Bracknell Referees' Association. I was then asked to referee a minimum of one game a month which I slotted into my itinerary. My Sunday League side packed up so Max and I founded a new club and called it Wescott as it seemed like a good idea to Max as Wescott Road was the central point where we tended to meet up in Wokingham before going out for our usual Friday or Saturday night evenings out. To spice things up I produced a programme for the team, Publicising this resolved a long running problem of lack of referees in the league. All newly appointed officials wanted to do our team to get their name in print. We hardly ever didn't have one after that. If one failed to turn up I was then qualified to take his place. Having a 100 club, Social Club and charging the players a signing on fee and a pay as you play fee made the club financially secure very quickly given that kit, balls and nets all had to be purchased. One of the players fathers Roger Wareham went to the extreme of videoing most matches. I still retain one tape of me in goal fumbling badly. I dropped back and played in goal for most of my appearances and it was the stuff nightmares were made of as the defence was non existent leading to me being kept very much occupied for most of the match. Scores of 11 - 2 against were not uncommon. Off the pitch the club went from strength to strength and after a successful Christmas Dinner at the local beefeater the club purchased pennants and pens. We became a senior club in every aspect off the park. Pity the displays didn't reflect the effort being shown behind the scenes. The programme was voted 3rd Nationally out of all Sunday League issues for which I received a trophy. Quite a few Sunday sides issue you would be surprised, I certainly was when I saw how many had entered.

Before a ball was kicked in anger, Redhill FC contacted me for help. The local council wanted Redhill's ground to be converted into offices and had agreed to resite them and erect floodlights. This left the club with a shortage of cash to rebuild their new ground. I was contacted for ideas which I duly sent by return and the grateful club awarded me with shares in Redhill FC, which I still retain.

My marks were good in the Sunday League and I was then asked to officiate in FA Competitions and in the Combined Counties League. I had over looked one small point. I was now playing and officiating on Saturdays and Sundays in the same two leagues. At first no problem, but being fairly strict I found if I had cautioned a player one week as referee I could be seriously tackled by him the following week whilst as a player. Saturdays in the Senior League I didn't have too much of a problem, but the Sunday games was a different matter especially with one team called Silver Birch after the pub from which the players drank in. In one match on 24th March I had to send off one player and caution three others. When the team turn up at 10.30 all ready drinking I knew I was in for a problem, but when they play with extra players who refuse to join the substitutes on the side and I send a player off for Foul and Abusive language only to find he had sneaked back on to the pitch again 10 minutes later. I had had enough. After threats of abandoning the match they behaved themselves. After the match I reported them to Peter Bentley as Referee Secretary who stopped me from reporting them to the FA. I processed the paperwork and both the League and FA took their own action with fines and bans. This unfortunately didn't stop me being "accidentally" kicked in my kneecaps when Wescott played them a few weeks later. At the end of the season I retained my Refereeing Certificate and stayed on for the Combined Counties League only for my own safety. Unfortunately by then the damage had been done and my knees were showing severe signs of fatigue and stress. It was not uncommon to lie on Teresa's bed on a Sunday afternoon doubled up in agony after a weekend of playing.

The season kicked off with a friendly at Wokingham, Phil had agreed to bring West Ham down to help boost the club financially. The game finished 4 - 3 in West Ham's favour. Cardiff City then returned to help Town after knocking them out of the FA Cup 1st Round last season. Town surprisingly won 2 - 1, and City featured a young Paul Bodin in its team that day. Then the match I tried to organise the previous season. Roy wanted a closer look at Cobham's training lights as he wanted some for Finchampstead Road. Both teams fielded their strongest sides with Wokingham winning 4 - 2. I was probably in the most neutral of positions being Senior Linesman! Wokingham had several changes in it. Paul Bence had left to manage Wycombe Wanderers and the former Portsmouth Fulham and QPR Player Ernie Howe had been drafted in to assist Roy with the coaching of the team and he had ideas to take the club places.

The next match was to be extremely memorable. I was playing for Cobham Reserves in a friendly against local side Emma Hamilton, near to half time one of the linesman injured himself and I found myself finishing off the match as linesman. I doubt if that has ever happened in senior football before! (Cobham lost 4 - 2 again for the record)

I then left for Holland after doing a programme to cover 5 matches whilst I was away. Henk met me at the airport as usual and What a trip that was. On the way out of the airport the exhaust fell off his Renault and we had to sit by the motorway for an hour and a half whilst help arrived. I got used to his taste in music by the end of the trip!

First stop was to rejoin Mike Small at Go Ahead Eagles, Henk had used his influence on his last trip to England to Bring Leicester City over for a tour. Gordon Milne, Steve Lynex and I got to know each other fairly well before both parties returned to the UK. Leicester won 4 - 1. One of the Eagles players was Eddie Bosman, whose brother was to throw the football world into turmoil a few years later. Next stop was Den Haag now that was a club. The fans had burnt down the club's main stand in defiance because they had been relegated from the Premier League to Division One. And critics say our fans have problems! This was their first match in the new Division but fortunately the game passed without incident as they drew with Eindhoven (PSV's poorer neighbours) 1 - 1.

I had to return to Feyenoord and Eric got tickets for their Annual Tournament. This time it was for the Final only and Feyenoord played before a capacity crowd who enjoyed watching the Dutch team beat Manchester United 1 - 0. Cruijff and Gullitt were at their best! I had a surprise the following evening as we returned to link up with Leicester City and whilst I was by the touch line talking with Steve Lynex a familiar face appeared out of the players tunnel with Gary Linekar it was Dean Wilkins. Steve called over and Gary introduced Dean to me. He had just signed for PEC Zwolle from Brighton and was to line up against Leicester in their friendly. Leicester won an entertaining match 3 - 2.

My playing was for one match only, having trained with Ajax I found myself facing them in a friendly for a non league club called Isselmeervogels. Ajax included Eddie's now famous brother John, Jan Molby, Ronald Koeman, Jesper Olson, and Frank Rijkaard yet we pulled off the shock of the season by winning 2 - 1. the Ajax Manager Aad de Mos was impressed and I was invited back for the Amsterdam Tournament, a few days later. Henk took me to Belgium to see a Belgian League match between SK Beveren and Beershot. SK won 3 - 1 and we returned to Holland. I found the country extremely dirty whether it was the region I don't know but I've never returned! Next on the list was NAC Breda beating Romanian side Sportul Bucharest 2 - 1 in a friendly and my introduction to proper Dutch food. Mayonnaise instead of chips I can live with, but raw herring in a buttered roll I found quite repulsive at first, but got used to it after a while. Next a bit of sight seeing was on the cards by request. Cheeses at Gouda then over to Germany and seeing a few castles. Henk hated that and wanted to see more grounds, we arranged to meet up several hours later. Bad Bochum is in North Germany near the Dutch border and my German is almost as bad as my Dutch so lunch was in an Italian Restaurant. I couldn't understand the menu so just pointed to something which looked good. The waiter smiled and brought me frogs legs. After working out how to get the meat off the legs I was pleasantly surprised the meat did taste like chicken! Payment was easy by handing over a credit card. So I survived my first trip alone just!

Then back to Amsterdam to rejoin Ajax for a spot of light training in a fenced off area in front of the club's ground. My knees started to give and I was viewed a risk and not signed. This was my first experience of playing the "Continental Style" properly! In this country it is purely 11 a side throughout all age groups but in Holland the youngsters start at 6 in 6 a side giving them more time on the ball to gain the skills needed for later on in life. This is now only starting to happen over here with the FA starting Mini Soccer schools which will probably start to be successful about the turn of the century. The

FA's first step to grow football players properly is coming across opposition in the old guard who coach the kids to win and for their own benefit rather than for the enjoyment of the sport and giving the children confidence which they badly need at that age. Also on the continent the players are rotated in their positions in training, as is so often the case in this country a full back gets lost when crossing the half way line as he is not used to playing out of position. Likewise forwards who come back to defend fail badly. This is why the Europeans beat us as they are used to playing in different positions to suit the game they are playing. By adapting to being in other places they are quicker to the ball as their confidence is high. For me it meant that instead of being bad in one position, I was terrible all over the park!

We watched the tournament which was staged at the old Olympic Stadium which held more than the old Ajax Stadium. Feyenoord lost 3 - 2 to Brazilian side Athletico Mineros and Ajax beat the Romanian National side 1 - 0.

Alkmaar was next as I hobbled out of the car. two matches were played in their annual open day. First was an old AZ '67 side against local side Zaanstreak. The veterans won 3 - 2. Immediately afterwards came AZ'67 against Mike Small and his Go Ahead Eagles side. A 2 - 2 followed.

My last day in Holland finished with a Dutch 1st Division match between Telstar and RKC which the home side won 2 - 0. then off to catch my flight home feeling totally exhausted. I needed rest on arrival back in Wokingham, but I was not to get it. Max dragged me to Stamford Bridge to see Chelsea's return to the 1st Division, Helicopters on the pitch and all the excitement went over my head as I sat back and saw Sunderland lose 1 - 0. I was glad to get home.

Eric then followed me over from Rotterdam and stayed with my parents for a few days. He wanted to go to Elm Park, so we went to see the 1 - 1 draw in the Milk Cup with Millwall. A draw was probably the best result possible for at half time some Millwall thugs broke into the stand and sat with the supporters. Eric and I shared our two seats with two thugs who were hiding from the police. It was a bit cramped but better than having my legs further injured as they were still very sore.

Getting back to Cobham was a bit of an anti climax after the previous fortnight. I was doing very light training and wasn't to be able to play for a few more weeks. So I took advantage of Peter Day's offer and obtained the promised complimentary tickets for their UEFA Cup match with Sporting Braga. Spurs won convincingly 6 -0 and I was to return the following week for Halifax's Milk Cup match, which Spurs won again very convincingly 4 - 0. Cobham reserves then won 6 - 1 against Ash United Reserves with my scoring on my return to action, morale victory over Dawn I thought.

Above: Wescott FC
Below: One of my Referees reports

B. & B. F.A./19

General Secretary:-
W. J. GOSLING
Tel: Faringdon (0367) 22099

COUNTY OFFICE,
15A LONDON STREET,
FARINGDON,
OXON. SN7 8AG

Nº 9525 (4)

Date: 28th March 1985

Dear Sir/Madam,

Bracknell Wanderers   v.   Silver Birch Reserves

in   John Wood Sunday League

played on   24th March 1985

I enclose a copy of the Referees' Report stating that during this match he cautioned your player(s).

DOBIN TIDY
NORMAN TIDY
SIMON LENNON

Note: When replying please advise if name(s) as shown above are correct; also confirm Christian Names.

I am instructed by the Disciplinary Committee of this Association to inform you that the incident(s) are to be placed on Record in the Association's Register for future reference and may be taken into account if any future misconduct by the player(s) occur. Will you please inform the player(s) of this action.

Your Club has been ordered to pay the Costs amounting to £15 in respect of this matter which should be paid to me within 21 days from date of this letter.

Attention is drawn to Regulation 15/70—Misconduct of Officials, Players and Spectators.

Yours faithfully,

General Secretary.

To: Hon. Secretary,
Silver Birch

This copy to be forwarded to Referee submitting original Report

Above: Training with Ajax. Can you spot me immediately to the trainers (yellow) right nearest the camera?
Below: Isselmeervogels v Ajax played at Amersfoort FC. Both taken by Henk.

Henk visited for a week, as he had shown me courtesy over the past two seasons I could not do anything other than let him stay with us. In return he drove me to watch two England games against Finland. First to Southampton for the Under 21's match which England won 2 - 0, then to Wembley the next day for the 5 - 0 victory in the World Cup Qualifying Round. Before he went home I accompanied him to Portsmouth where he wanted to meet an old friend Les Allen which we did prior to a tour round the ground.

I had the weekend off so went to Highbury with Andrew Lewington. Andrew was an Estate Agent who played football for Wescott worse than I did! I bumped into him in 1994 and was pleased to note I had more hair than him. He was losing it rapidly. Whereas I had taken an interest in Ice Hockey, he had gone to Basketball and was a qualified coach coaching the Bracknell National side the Thames Valley Tigers and the Junior England team. He was an Arsenal supporter so the Sunderland match was a good one to choose as it was the first ever match when a club had experimented with TV screens. It was a weird experience to see it. The experiment lasted a month before being removed. These days it is common at most Premier League grounds. Arsenal won 3 - 2 through goals by Caton, Allinson and Talbot.

Bracknell Town were drawn against Chalfont St Peter in the 2nd Round of the Berks. & Bucks Cup so I made my first visit to watch the team I was Vice President of. My former team won 3 - 1 to take the shine off the evening.

Next stop was White Hart Lane as Max wanted to see the 1 - 1 draw with Chelsea and then being on standby for Phil Parkes who had organised a charity match. His eleven beat a select side 8 - 1 with out my involvement.

Boxing Day is traditionally the day over Christmas when my family get together. This year I decided I wanted to go to Loftus Road to see QPR draw 2 - 2 with Chelsea. I have yet to live it down and even today get a comment thrown at me in jest from my Aunt Eileen that I put my friends before my family. Never again was I to go to a match and avoid the gathering.

The Kings Road pubs again beckoned on New Years Day when Nottingham Forest visited Stamford Bridge. The Blues won 1 - 0 but I couldn't drink too much as I was back in training again. A victory over Fleet and then losing to Hartley Wintney came and went without much incident and I then found I was selected to officiate at Wokingham Town. Linesman for the team's reserve match against British Aerospace in the 2nd Round of the Southern Combination Cup which Town won 3 - 2.

Cobham had contacts in Fleet Street. The Daily Mail's Racing Correspondent Jim Stanford was a regular fixture at the clubhouse bar. However, the Daily Express played an annual friendly against their Belgian colleagues at the Gazette Van Antwerpen. This year was the 25th Anniversary of the match and it was to be played in England and Cobham was selected to stage the event. Chris Bird the Cobham physio was asked to guest in goal, his first time in goal since facing a penalty shoot-out against that elephant from the previous season. I was asked to take one of the lines for the 0 - 0 draw, which I accepted. The Expresses General Manager Mr Dennis then presented everyone with a small trophy to commemorate the event. I produced a programme for the event which went down well. My engraved prize can still be seen behind the bar at the club. I accidentally left it behind on the day and it was commandeered and put in a prominent place as the front featured the Express logo and was to be a feature point by the till. I got to see it regularly as after training I usually did a stint of bar work on a Tuesday night to give barman Dave Short a break.

About 12 months previously Harrods suffered a bomb blast, one of its victims was Policeman Jon Gordon. Chalfont's President David Pembrooke decided to help him and contacted the Watford Manager Graham Taylor for his help. The result was a Benefit match at the Playing Fields when Graham lived up to his promise and brought the entire first team. The club also used the occasion to open their new clubhouse. The 2 - 0 victory to the Hornets was immaterial as a capacity crowd turned up to help Jon who was very appreciative of what is now in the club record books as their record attendance.

**Above: My Families
club Chalfont St Peter**

**Right: Fred Latham
Senior One of the
Founders of the club.**

81

After the match I joined the Watford team in the clubhouse for a buffet. Graham made a wonderful speech and made a further donation to the funds by presenting a cheque to Jon on behalf of the Watford players for £500. My colleague Andy Thomas at ICI who had got me the job in Sales was a loyal Watford supporter so as he could not make the match I asked Graham Taylor if he could sign a programme for him as a gesture of thanks. I mentioned my visit to Wembley to see the team play, he smiled and took the programme away and came back a few minutes later with the team captain Wilf Rostron who had just finished making a speech and to my surprise I was given two programmes signed by the entire squad. I found both Luther Blissett and John Barnes very approachable and enjoyed the time spent with them.

At the end of the season scandal ensued at Chalfont with one of the committee members who was very well known to my family then left her husband and ran off with a fellow committee member. The club tried to cover up the embarrassment and dissolved the committee and Vice Presidents in favour of Directors. I was not prepared to commit any more money to the club and was dropped from the officials list.

The Continentals had split up and reformed as the Dutchies. Henk and Jan came over and visited several grounds. I accompanied them to the Manor Ground to see Oxford United beat Middlesbrough 1 - 0. The main reason for their interest was the Middlesbrough player Hiene Otto who was Dutch. We all chatted and had our photos taken before retiring to the players Lounge were a "Dutchies Clog" was presented to the club. This can still be seen in the trophy cabinet between the two bars in the players lounge. I caught up with Maurice Evans again who by now was Chief Scout at Oxford. He confirmed his interest in going to Wokingham and prising Bobby Saunders and Steve Butler away from Roy. Steve was still in the army which led to problems but Maurice was trying to get him to try out in a reserve match. He was too late as Brentford came in for him and bought him out of the military. Steve went from strength to strength with Brentford before going onto Watford, Maidstone and now

Gillingham. Wokingham finished on a high by defeating Chesham United 1 - 0 to lift the Berks. & Bucks. Cup again.

My season finished by paying my respects to Pat Jennings who was retiring. Arsenal played a testimonial match with Tottenham who won 3 - 2 in front of over 25, 000 fans.

The Tottenham connection did not end there that season as Danny Blanchflower was the Guest of Honour at Cobham's Annual Dinner Dance. I was duly presented with another trophy as a result of the programme's success. The most eventful year of my career then drew to a close.

Chapter 9
Another Sunday and Sweet FA

Having received another honour for Wescott's programme The content was improved as I went for number one nationally for Sunday clubs. However, I was not too see the season out with them. The players started to object to my bringing in two new players with learning difficulties. I had been approached by the local school who wished to see these two teenagers play regularly. They were a little slow but had talent, so I agreed to do my bit for the community. One of those two repaid my faith in him, Rob McKay later went on to Captain England in the Alternative European Championships in England in 1996. This was set up for Nations with footballers with learning difficulties. After problems with the team over non payment of fees I decided I had had enough hassle and accepted an offer to move up three Divisions to be Player Manager of FC Bracknell. Programmes were issued and I had the honour of being placed twice in the top three of the annual awards that season. Issue number one was for a friendly I had organised at Palmer Park Sports Stadium in Reading under floodlights against my colleagues from Cobham. I faced my Cobham colleagues and played probably the worst game of my life much to the amusement of most of the Cobham officials who had come along for the spectacle. Bracknell won 2 - 1 thanks to Jason Parker restoring my self esteem. Cobham fielded their new signing Steve Kember, the former Chelsea player who signed direct from Crystal Palace and remained at Palace to train whenever possible. A truly dedicated player. And Stuart Nichol a former Tranmere Rovers player and England Schoolboy.

The club had three teams and were even better run than Wescott with committee meeting held monthly. Social events were a priority including evenings out a Blazers in Windsor for an Evening with

Jimmy Tarbuck and Kenny Lynch boosting club funds more that signing on fees.

The players were a great bunch in the Pub but regularly got drunk and slept in on a Sunday so missing kick off. I ended up bringing in my own team, several from Wescott and Jason in from the first team. My playing career improved by playing Centre Forward and Right Wing and I scored with an unusual frequency.

The end of season presentation Evening was an event not to be missed. I was runner up to Russell Gore as Clubman of the Year and the speech I gave was to some extent different. Teresa's comments afterwards were that it wasn't me. I still don't know what she meant! I was awarded the League's Sportsman's award which was an honour I was very proud of.

The serious Stuff on the Saturday side started with a friendly at home to Redhill, I played in the scoreless draw on the understanding I assisted David Dobinson the League's Referee's Secretary, who had now joined the committee at Cobham.

A spying mission to see Town lose 2 - 1 to Brentford did not inspire the Cobham team, who promptly lost to Wokingham 2 - 0. I was again running along the touchline as senior Linesman (sorry Referee's Assistant if you comply with FIFA's new regulations!).

Above: FC Bracknell
Below: Regaining my scoring touch!

I was given unlimited access to the photocopier so went to town. I was asked for humour well they got it. Cobham programmes became books! The price was increased to 25p but with a minimum of 32 pages, but normally over 40 and occasionally reaching 60 plus these programmes quickly became sort after and after programme subscriptions were taken into account, we sold out most weeks. Each time we increased production, sales rose. It was their best season for making a profit The club had to return to Roy during the season to reprint the glossy programme covers.

Bob Freeland announced his retirement from the committee at the end of the season so I felt it should not pass without being recognised. Being a Spurs supporter I contacted Peter Barnes Tottenham's Assistant Secretary to arrange a friendly. Due to commitments it was not possible to arrange so Peter and I set up something else for later in the season.

Cobham went to Hampton for a pre season friendly. I was not selected to play, so spent the match sitting alongside writer Allan Simpson of Steptoe and Son fame. He was Hampton's President and took delight in seeing his side steamroller over my bunch 5 - 1. Two more appearances for the reserves proceeded an invitation from Slough Town to guest for them in a charity match against an All Stars side. I readily accepted, but didn't play on the day as my knees were again playing up and badly I was seeing the beginning of the end of my playing career! I watched the 3 - 3 draw from the bench.

Work with ICI was now taking off, I was given my own promotional budgets which my Store Managers were more than happy to try to spend for me. Sandfords (Since taken over by Texas) were the most receptive and the High Wycombe branch next to the former Wycombe Wanderers ground took several promotion including coasters and Dog and Girl events. This later became known as Dog and Dog events due to the mental state of some of the models we employed. ICI had 9 different Old English Sheepdogs which they called upon for TV and physical appearances. So obtaining "Duke" was not a problem and the events proved very popular The kids had their photos taken with the dog whilst mums did the shopping and dads looked at the non furry dog. I was lucky to obtain the services of Suzy Mitzi for one store opening. She was a particularly attractive page 3 model, who was different. She had a brain. I was pleasantly surprised on how intelligent she was and enjoyed the day with her immensely. The resultant sales and sold in Gondola ends of paint meant I achieved my targets in style. Being stitched up the following year I still won 3rd Place in ICI's Sales man of the year, just piped by my old mate Andy Thomas. The Paints Division were not backward in rewarding this achievement. Both Teresa and I joined with Andy and his girlfriend along with some of the top brass for an evening out in Bournemouth at a luxury hotel followed by awards of Porcelain crockery and a canteen of cutlery presented in an expensive table. Worth over £300. Ideal considering I was collecting for my bottom drawer as I was to get married the following year. I never used the gifts though and they still remain with me as a reminder of happy times in the past. Being stopped for speeding on the M3 on the way home left a bitter taste in the mouth though.

I wandered up to Wembley to see England draw 1 - 1 with Rumania in the World Cup Qualifying match. A stark difference to officiating the following day at Larges Lane. Bracknell Town's reserve team won 8 - 1 against Waltham St Lawrence in a cup match, this was not to be the highest score at a match I officiated at during the season!

Steve Aldham had been transferred to Chertsey Town from Wokingham so I was now to play against my old friend. I turned up to see the side thrash Westfield 5 - 1 with Steve in sparkling form. The next time I was to appear at the ground would be under completely different circumstances.

Turkey was next on the menu and having seen England stuff them 5 - 0 it was back to Anvil Lane for FA Vase action. The club had never reached the 2nd Round in its history so to win 2 - 1 was a complete shock not only to the team, but to the opposition Horndean as well.

The club did a prediction League and I predicted Oxford United to get to the Milk Cup Final, only to lose to Chelsea. Winning against QPR was close but at least I correctly guessed their path. Manchester United were to win the league and Arsenal the FA Cup. I was nearly right!

I incorporated cartoon characters of personalities in the club like Michelle Hills who was always changing her hair style or make up. Everyone joined in the fun and probably the funniest programme in England resulted. Michelle was not always too appreciative though and Liz who worked behind the bar and did most of the photocopying took over, she got her own back by making her own comments in an issue after I had given the hard copy of the programme to her for copying. I can look back and say quite categorically that this was the happiest season of my career!

A major move around occurred when Fleet played Ash I was in attendance with 6 other league referees who discussed the current state of the game and why FC Bracknell had paid £5 to Wescott as a transfer fee for me. A free Transfer or a large fee is acceptable, but I could never accept £5 which seemed a bit of an insult. Dawn Reynolds then appeared to say she was leaving Ash and David was leaving Fleet to return to Chalfont, I ended up leaving the ground in a state of confusion. David was not present when Fleet returned for a league match a few week's later.

Malden Vale Reserves against Farnham Town Reserves will always stick in my mind as being linesman my tie ups fell off and I couldn't find them. The referee's assessor was present and approached the referee and myself at half time to correct the matter. I played the second half with miles of cellotape wrapped round the black socks and still they fell down before the final whistle.

Shock Horror! Cobham then hit a winning streak and beat Ringmer 1 - 0 to reach the 3rd round of the FA Vase, Local press and County Radio took a lot of interest and all of a sudden publicity which led to increased attendance's. However, the 3rd Round was as far as the club went as they exited 4 - 0 at the hands of Abingdon Town at Anvil Lane. The club President Michael Dennis who managed the Daily Express side the previous year went so far as to give the club coverage in the paper. Praise in deed!

ICI then had their annual sales conference which proved to be a typical sales do. After watching Selina Scott doing the usual presentation type bit where most fell asleep, The Sheraton Skyline at Heathrow provided a band to play whilst we had drinks by the pool bar. The Baron Knights then appeared to spark the evening off, and then the Paints Division made a mistake FREE BAR ALL NIGHT! The Scots ended up being sent to bed at midnight for being drunk and disorderly, I fell in the pool fully clothed. Whilst the salesman I ended up sharing a room with was last seen wandering up the A4 looking for a Taxi. Rob Finch later made amends by beating both Andy and I to the Salesman of the Year title.

Cars became a talking point, I damaged mine reversing into playing colleague Andy Bell's car virtually writing it off, but the best one went to Andy's brother Nick who demolished the home dug out by reversing his Capri into it one Saturday evening after a match. As a result of my misdemeanour I involved another player Trevor Foster in my plans for Bob Freeland.

As Tottenham could not fulfil a testimonial fixture with us Peter Barnes invited three of us to White Hart Lane for the League match with Ipswich Town on 21st December, Trevor drove. On arrival we were taken in the lift which we shared with the actor Warren Mitchell to the Oak Room where a free drink was waiting for us before taking our seats in the West Stand. Half time was tea in the Oak Room, before watching the second half. After Final whistle we were joined by Bobby Robson (England Manager at that time) Sir Stanley Rous and Pat Jennings in the Oak Room who chatted for a while over drinks. Once Peter had completed his duties a tour of the Dressing Rooms Executive and Directors Boxes before walking onto the pitch. Whilst Bob was still enjoying his day out we joined the players in the players lounge who presented him with a club diary, handbook and pen. It was a day he will never forget and Peter did us proud!

I had by now established a routine to my week at work and knew on a Thursday I would be starting the day at Homecharm in Witney and the manager David Waite (brother of Terry) would have the kettle on by the time I had arrived. Then it was off to Wantage then Oxford. On route was breakfast normally a bacon sandwich in a lay by on the A40. Terry had just been kidnapped and David quite rightly had other things on his mind so I didn't stay long or have my usual cuppa and made for my usual lay-by. The caravan was there as normal so I pulled in. A man and a woman were inside having breakfast so I opened the door and asked for a cup of tea and a bacon sandwich. The gentleman gave me a funny look so I repeated my request. Again he looked totally surprised. I said

"This is the tea bar isn't it?"

to which the response came

"no".

Apparently the normal caravan had moved on and this couple were touring and had parked in the same spot. They made me a cup of tea, but I've been cautious about eating out ever since!

I surpassed that by going to watch Abingdon Town play a few weeks later and parked in the rugby club next door by mistake and wondering why with 20 minutes to go to kick off no one was around or any lights were on. I gave up and went home missing their game with Hounslow.

On returning from the Spurs match I embarked on a month of playing 4 games and officiating on a further 2. The games at Cove and Chobham were fairly easy games to referee, but the home game with Ash was a different story with a convincing 4 -0 defeat. I met up again with Glenn Hoddle at Wokingham when the Spurs team played a friendly and drew 1 - 1. This was a favour returned for earlier helping provide the opposition at White Hart Lane at short notice to test Glenn's fitness prior to an important match. Roy was more than happy to see over 1, 300 people turn out and boost the clubs takings.

The weather claimed a few fixtures in February and I gladly took up an opportunity to train with Blackburn Rovers on the 20th. Blackburn were to have played Fulham the following day and came down on the Wednesday to stop over at the nearby Severn Hills Hotel. Like Liverpool had done the previous year, they requested somewhere to train and were pointed in Cobham's direction. But unlike Liverpool who just turned up and ruined the pitch without permission, Blackburn were very polite and courteous. I was invited to join in and readily accepted as I had done earlier in the season when I assisted Huddersfield Town with their set pieces prior to their F A Cup match at Reading.

Cobham were stripped of nine league points by the Surrey County FA in January after they fielded Mickey Follett, a player suspended at the end of last season for being sent off at Malden Town. Cobham Manager Dave Tippett's excuse was

"Follett played for Cobham last year before I came here. I brought the squad together for pre season training and he came along unaware of the ban. He played in our opening three league games before someone asked us if we knew we were fielding a suspended player. I feel that although rules are rules, this was a genuine error down to the committee at Cobham. I'm very disappointed because the team is innocent, but now all their hard work is down the drain. We still had as good a chance as anyone of winning the league, and with so long to go I could have fancied our chances. We have now just got to get on with it and build for next season".

As a committee member I was unaware of this and came as a shock to see Dave's comments in print. He was of course right. Those 9 points would have made a lot of difference.

As a result of the postponements in February, the final two months of the season became a nightmare, forgetting about work I had to play and officiate twice a week for 8 weeks and fit in programme production as well. That spell finished me as a player! Oxford City against Bracknell in the AC Delco Cup was no problem as I had been working in Oxford that day and found the old ground very easily. But Frimley Green v Ash quickly followed by appearing at the Reserves v Farnham as Senior Linesman then Ash United v Cove in quick succession caused my knees to tweak again even though I was not playing. I found time to attend the Arsenal v Watford 1st Division match to try to relax and the Aldershot defeat by Hartlepool, but found it difficult to sit still for more than 20 minutes without moving around.

Back to Ash United to run the line for their reserve match with Merstham then Farnham v Frimley Green. I rested my knees from playing the rest of the season with FC Bracknell and it helped me survive the final few weeks. 19th April appeared and I went back to Ash who were getting very used to me by now. To say the game was so one sided would be an understatement. I had virtually nothing to do in the second half and found myself talking to a small band of fans on the half way line who had recognised me from previous weeks. I kept my back to them so I could continue watching for an off side which never came. The final whistle sounded and Ash United had beaten Fleet Town 11 - 0!

Three final games for Cobham then came up. Being a bench warmer for all three. I missed a 4 - 1 victory over Horley Town; a 5 - 4 victory over Ash United and worst of all a 3 - 0 victory over Godalming Town Reserves in the Combined Counties League Reserve Cup at Chertsey. Even Steve Aldham came over to watch me. Being on the bench I still received a winners trophy but would have preferred to have contributed to the success.

The end of season Dinner Dance was one of celebration having won a trophy for the first time in years. The programme had finished 2nd in the league under Ash United and a very creditable 17th nationally. I forgot to enter our Reserve team programme in the new category as this was as good as for 1st team matches. I would have won that category, still I wasn't greedy! We scored 111 points as opposed to Ash's 120 the top reserve issue was awarded 80. Even Wescott got 98 in coming 2nd in the Sunday Section. Top of the pile was Braintree with 165 points, 23 in front of Lancing then it was very close for the rest of us.

My knees now finished, Teresa finally won her battle and persuaded me to retire from Semi Professional football and I stood down at the club's Annual Dinner Dance. John Hollins was doing the honours as guest speaker this year and was very entertaining. He obviously had a set script, but he took time before the meal to find out a bit about the team and used their names in the speech. Even Teresa enjoyed it which is something for someone who hates the sport! John did all the end of season presentations including making a presentation to me.

Work was now concentrating me in the area from High Wycombe to Oxford so with the hanging up of my boots came my resignation from the committee and the programme. I regretted that move, but paid employment had to come before a small win bonus as a player. John Hamon took over as Editor assisted by his wife Sue. John had plenty of experience working on Shoot magazine so I left the programme in good hands.

Chapter 10
Offside

1986 - 87 season started as usual with pre season training at FC Bracknell, and my knees felt reasonably good. After watching Wokingham beat Wimbledon 6 - 1 in a friendly I quickly drove up the road to Larges Lane to take control of the Bracknell v Thanet United friendly, which was more a kick about as it was both sides first match and both teams were not fully fit. Bracknell won 1 - 0 and I was asked to come back and run the line for their next friendly against Bournemouth as one of the other officials had dropped out, I accepted. My knees started to twitch quite badly during the league side's 2 - 0 victory, so afterwards made a request to the Berks. and Bucks. FA to be put on the Referee's non active list for the foreseeable future. This was readily agreed to and I was able to rest for as long as required. ICI then confirmed to me that I had to make a decision as to my football career or work career as it was made more than plain to me that I would not be allowed any time off work for operations. Work won and I stopped training.

Not training left me a little unfit, but I managed to survive one last season in the Sunday League. We got through three strips that season as players kept "Misplacing" their shirts after threats of fines failed to produce the kit that had been "left behind by accident and someone else picked it up" excuses arose. The Sponsor Pat Cavner who ran his own sports shop in Bracknell provided one last kit which I guarded throughout the rest of the season. The social aspect flourished with discos and another successful evening at Blazers to see Duncan Norvelle, in fact 500 tickets were sold to boost club funds for the trip to Windsor. The 100 club became the 200 club The first game in and the team had won 3 - 0 to go top of the league, things were going very well. The problems of the previous year then re emerged and I found myself short of players and having to play myself.

The Annual ICI Sales Conference took me back to Scotland and

Gleneagles. Whilst it was strictly business it was noticed that a few colleagues had smuggled their golf clubs onto the plane. Like last year every thing was free. The drinks on the plane combined with the high altitude meant most were feeling ill by the time we arrived. Roy Hudd was the compare this year and his repertoire was extremely blue and not to the taste of some of my female colleagues. Haggis was on the menu piped in by the drummers, most avoided it, but I find it quite enjoyable in small doses. One thing I did notice was the extorsionate prices of all the goods in the Hotel. A polo shirt for myself, a tie for my dad and a few bits for Teresa cost me nearly £50. Nice place to visit but I won't be going there again!

Chris Nixon is a qualified Dentist in Bracknell with his own successful business. The Combined Counties League used to pair us up quite frequently as we lived close to each other and could share transport and keep expenses down. Chris drove in his new BMW most of the time after I scared him on the way back from a game at Malden Vale when I nearly put my company car into the crash barrier on the A3 after a lorry had refused me right of way at a junction. He enjoyed telling the story at the Bracknell branch of the Referee's Association so I took revenge in the programme when he was selected to referee one of my team's matches. He never took the Michael again!

Christmas 1986 saw me reluctantly stand down as manager due to mounting work pressures and my knees finally giving out. The team was still placed in the top three in the league and doing very well under my guidance and I handed all duties over to Russell Gore. Apathy followed after I had left and the club slid down the table. At the end of season Presentation Evening the club merged with the other two senior teams and ceased to exist. I was even more surprisingly voted Clubman of the year, the Shield I still have with the rest of my football trophies on display in my house.

I took one of my customers to the Reading v Arsenal F A Cup 3rd Round tie, which was one of the coldest days I can ever remember. Dad had a handwarmer he used for golf and we borrowed that to try to keep us warm. Arsenal winning 3 - 1 in front of the Match of the Day cameras.

Not being able to play was frustrating and going to matches tended to have me wishing I was involved so with plans going ahead for my wedding in October, work and searching for somewhere to live I only went to one further match all season. That was Wycombe Wanderers Berks. & Bucks Cup Semi Final at Loakes Park when Wycombe won 5 - 1 against Abingdon Town. The reason I did that was I was working late and Sandford's car park was next to the club so I stayed on for the match.

Work did not ease up but I was awarded top place in the newly designed Salesman of the Quarter awards twice in a row. Then disaster I fell fowl of an over ambitious B & Q Manager who was seeking to further his own means and I got involved in an internal battle which to my amazement ICI decided that B & Q were to big a customer to risk arguing with and sided with him. I was disgusted at being dictated to and resigned. Being a few weeks before my wedding was probably not the best of moves but I did some work with some old friends from my days as a shop manager. Tony Angus and Jason Parker had opened their own chain of shops and I assisted them until I sorted myself out with another job.

The Stag Night was unforgettable for most, I can't really remember much at all as my lagers were spiked and I was later told I was dragged from pub to pub throughout Wokingham drinking double scotches. All I can recall was my brother Paul helping to carry me home. I was so bad I had alcohol poisoning at my wedding!

Chapter 11

A Move, A Marriage, And A Murder

I had been put in the horrendous position of being made my brother's Best Man when he had married earlier in the year, I was known for my wit and sense of humour so was pressed to do the job, however, standing in front of all my relatives all staring at me my mind went blank in panic and the speech I had thought up went out of my head completely. Having suffered this mishap I was better prepared for the next attempt. Standing at the church still feeling the worse for the stag night I became oblivious to everyone standing behind me and tried to keep a straight face as the person who was about to marry Teresa and I was called John Thomas and all sort of visions were going through my head. Teresa was the worst in sniggering as she said
"I take Stuart Dudley".
That bit over then came the boring session with camera's flashing all over the place before being rescued for the reception. Jason proved to be the Best BestMan I could have wanted. We had known each other for quite a few years and only attended his wedding to Mandy a few months earlier. Having worked and played football with him for a long time the speech was to everyone's expectations even if it was very embarrassing
"I know Stuart has played in every position, but I'm sure he will score tonight!"
had even my Grandmother in stitches. Thanks mate!

After a honeymoon in Spain it was back to Swindon. We found house prices too expensive in Wokingham and did not particularly like Bracknell so moved up the M4 a few junctions. We settled in West Swindon and still live there today, even if it is in different houses!

Henk came over for a trip prior to the wedding and kidnapped me for the day, taking me to see a friendly at Brighton with Bournemouth winning 2 - 0. Unknown to me at that time was his contacts extended to Swindon, and not long after I had moved in I received a letter from George Ranson, the Programme Editor at Hellenic League side Supermarine, so named after the former Vickers factory that was in Swindon that made Spitfires during the last war. I had now settled into a job selling DIY items for a wholesaler and establishing myself very well during the week and had weekends to spare. Teresa was not too happy! I wondered up for their 3 - 1 victory over Sharpness on 28th November and was amazed to find out just how much George knew about me and had told the committee. I was then talked into assisting George on the programme and joining the committee. Teresa went berserk! She didn't have that many friends at the time so looked forward to the weekends with me. Knowing how involved I get she was about to become a football widow after two months of marriage.

A murder had been committed in Swindon on 14th November, when a 17 year old Plymouth Argyle supporter was attacked in Gladstone Street, just off Manchester Road after his team had just played Swindon Town at the County Ground. He later died from injuries. Teresa had started to wonder what sort of town we had moved to and put pressure on me not to go. We resolved the problem, by taking an interest in Ice Hockey together, So my schedule would be to arrive at the club, put up the nets and do general duties. If lucky I would watch the first half of the match then join her to go to the Link Centre. In principle this worked until John Fisher who was one of the players suggested I start training with the team as I was around on Tuesday nights for committee meetings and handling programme articles etc. with George. My knees were rested and I felt no immediate effects when running so I accepted and trained with Peter Dearlove a young player who was on Torquay United's books as a 16 year old before thinking he was too good for them and was promptly released.

I resided with the reserve team, but as pains started to reappear I took not real part on the playing side, but formed a bond with the squad, who felt cut off from the first team. The club had sold its ground and now Pentel have an office on the spot were the clubhouse was. The pitch is now unused by BOC on the South Marston Industrial Estate. The landlords paid for the club to be moved 100 yards north to by the roundabout leading into the estate. Apart from the stand which moved with the club, everything else including the floodlights were new and provided by the landlords as the farm land was cheaper for them and selling the existing club land on the industrial estate brought in a huge profit. Given the new luxury settings a power struggle was starting to appear at the club and the back stabbing and internal politics were worse that any office within a large company. I let George do most of the first team programmes and concentrated myself on doing an issue for the Reserves. This helped in the bonding process between the two teams, but off it was a different matter.

George now saw his place as Editor under threat and started a few noises in the right direction to try to maintain his dominance. I had and never intended to take over. If I had life at home would have been unbearable! The fact that the end of the season saw us both being recognised in the annual programme awards seemed to count for nothing. He wanted all the glory.

Robbie Allen, the Chairman was empire building and causing a few headaches at committee meetings as he fought for supremacy. The unfortunate bystander being the Secretary Eric Stott who was probably the nicest person anyone could wish to meet.

To relieve the pressure I was now getting I paid my first visit to the County Ground to see Town beat Bournemouth 4 - 2 in the 2nd Division. This was the calm before the storm as I fell out with the Wiltshire FA. The Berks. & Bucks FA contacted me to say that although I was still registered with them it must now cease as I was living outside of their counties and to contact the Wilts FA in Faringdon and transfer my registration. I duly did so and was asked to referee an Hellenic League match. I informed them that I was currently inactive due to injury and on the Non Active list. The response from the Wiltshire FA was amazing. The letter I received was blunt and to the point. They do not recognise a non active list and if I was unprepared to referee their designated matches then I would not be allowed to keep my registration. The Berks. and Bucks FA were unable to help as I wished to retain the qualification and intended to continue to pay my fees, so I ceased to be a referee. By now I was starting to lose my appetite for the game because of bureaucracy.

I was given a ticket for the Littlewoods Cup Final between Arsenal and Luton Town which I took up. Despite losing 3 - 2 I enjoyed the game and a spark still existed inside me for the sport.

A polite but true review of all the Hellenic League club programmes were featured in the Supermarine programme, just as I had done at all my previous clubs with teams in their respective divisions without any trouble. I was verbally attacked by Robbie Allen for criticising the other clubs, no one else raised any objections from either the club's themselves or from our committee. Peter Dearlove had had enough and left to join Cirencester Town. Robbie went into hospital having suffered kidney stone problems. I told myself this was probably the reason he was publicly slating everyone. His return did not bring about any change in his temperament unfortunately. The final straw came at the final home game of the season against Pegasus Juniors in the Hellenic League. After assisting to put the nets up, ensure the programme was on sale and having watched 45 minutes of the game, I went to leave, Robbie came running up to me and said.

"Where do you think you are going?"

I turned round and told him

"I have promised to take my wife to an Ice Hockey match at the Link Centre."

To which his reply was:

"If you can't be bothered to watch all of the game then you can't be bothered with this club!"

I told him

"I had turned up to do the dirty work so why be like this?"

There was no reasoning with him, so I left and sent Eric a letter of resignation. I had had enough of being a pawn in this battle. Eric responded with a very polite letter accepting my resignation. Reading between the lines I think he knew the real reasons why I quit. Not long after George and several other members of the committee also turned their back on the politics and joined local rivals Highworth Town. George unfortunately died two years ago after dedicating his life to the sport. He will be sadly missed!

I then had a break from football for three seasons still highly disillusioned with the politics I had endured. Over the three years I only saw three matches. Arsenal's 2 - 2 draw with Charlton being the best remembered one, for several fantastic goals scored by both sides. The best one falling to Steve Mackenzie of Charlton. The other two being Swindon Reserves beating Charlton 3 - 2 in the Combination and a return to Finchampstead Road for an FA Trophy match which Wokingham drew with Merthyr Tydfil 2 - 2.

Work had been a source of change over the three years as well. Having done all I could with the wholesaler I handed my job over to former Portsmouth player Dean Fosbury, who was currently playing for Bognor Regis Town. After I had fully trained him, I left to go into business with my Father in Law. In hindsight this was a bad mistake, as one of the contracts we had at a local hotel conned us as the main contractor we were working for schemed behind our backs and we lost money owed to us by the £ thousands. We had no redress as a small un noticed clause in the contract allowed the contractor to get away with it! After going several months without a wage to make up for the loss, I left to work back in sales with Coca Cola. I was left with debts following this venture including my personal credit cards which were used to provide company equipment. Not only did I get left to sort out repayment on that, my Father in Law then decided to shed his responsibilities and go personally bankrupt. He walked away from it all. He went personally bankrupt instead of taking the company and as such stuck two fingers up at me. After his three years were up as a bankrupt, I was by then separated from Teresa and he made no effort to help me in all that time to clear the company debts. All the debtors were after payment from me as it was a partnership including the Inland Revenue chasing me for his unpaid tax. Teresa couldn't care less as she was by now living with someone else and trying to start a new life with her new husband and my kids so it was left to, me to clear little by little.

At Coke I was successful and exceeded my targets of selling in 22 Coke vending machines in each 4 week sales period and found myself constantly in the top 10 of salesmen out of the 72 strong vending division, called Vendleader. I made one special friend who has remained close to me ever since. Kirstine Bayliss, is a very attractive young lady who is 3 months younger than me. we would always be in touch with each other and to say Teresa was jealous would be an understatement. However, we had a party in Birmingham paid for by Vendleader when partners were invited and the pair got to meet each other properly. It was to be an eventful weekend as overnight a heavy snowfall had cut off most of the Midlands and we booked out of the hotel in a desperate bid to reach Teresa's parents who were babysitting for our son, Christopher. We eventually reached the roundabout by the motorway before becoming stuck. After about 4 hours in the car, I fortunately had a shovel in the boot and dug a route onto the roundabout and pushed the car onto it and abandoned it. Teresa was desperate to go to the toilet and ended up being covered by me as she christened the snow. Cold and embarrassed we walked the 2 miles back to the hotel and found we were unable to get our room back as someone else had taken it. Kirstine and her boyfriend at that time Steve, then offered the use of their room to shower and warm up. Teresa was by now not quite so hostile to Kay and they seemed to learn to accept each other. The weather lifted the following day and we managed to retrieve the car and make it home. Christopher was extremely pleased to see us both and showed it by bursting into tears at the sight of us arriving. Shortly afterwards both Kay and I had car phones installed in case an emergency cropped up again. Fortunately it never did! As Coca Cola were very strong on American tactics they were pleased that our group had bonded well, but they refused to pay for the second night's accommodation.

As most people can remember where they were when news of

President Kennedy's assassination was announced in the 1960's, likewise all football supporters can remember the moments on the 15th April 1989 when the horrors of Hillsborough were revealed! I was at home with Teresa and two friends Gary and Karen Taylor who were Reading Season Ticket holders, they had popped over with a birthday card for me a few days late. What was to be a quick visit turned into a long stay as we all sat down in disbelief at what was emerging on the TV screen as Grandstand kept returning to update their viewers on the horrors that were occurring. From the abandonment of Liverpool's FA Cup Semi Final with Nottingham Forest after six minutes following crushing at the Leppings Lane end of the stadium, to the final figure of 96 supporters dead. This worried Teresa even more about safety and I was not to go to another match until September 1991.

By then after a reorganisation at Coca Cola had turned 5 sales forces into 3, I left to start up my own company, which for two years were exclusively attached to Mates. I was initially one of four Business Development Managers, but this changed due to success and I was promoted to National Account Manager.

Going round the pubs and clubs selling condoms left me open to all types of jokes, eventually I became used to all the one liners thrown at me and developed my own responses. Being someone big in condoms was to be an exhilarating experience! I often found myself in awkward situations and being chatted up in gay pubs whilst trying to sell in the super strength condoms, but these guys normally backed off politely when they realised I was not that way inclined and only in the pub on business. However mistakes can also happen on my part! I met this gorgeous blonde in Swindon in a club after I had separated from my wife years later, her name was Julia. One thing led to another and by the time we had got back to her house and were in her bedroom I found that Julia was in fact a Julian. I have never moved so fast in my life to gather my clothes and run out of a house before! I let this bit out at a neighbours house one evening and it was over heard by another neighbour Tony who then everytime the neighbours have a

Above: Before the politics at Supermarine FC
Below: A new venture in life Ice Hockey with the Swindon Wildcats

get together likes to bring up the event to embarrass me in front of any guests I may bring along. I normally give as good as I get and a good natured verbal battle normally ensues with me winning most times, much to the amusement of all in attendance. Tony has since quietened down since his son let out a secret that he dresses up in his wife's dress to be the tooth fairy whenever any of the kids teeth fall out. Game, set and match to yours truly! Promotion up the ranks led me more into time management and fixed appointments and a little spare time. Companies like First Leisure in London and Apollo Leisure in Oxford became regular lines in my appointments diary. By chance I started to feel the need to see football again and called at several clubs to sell not only the condoms, but the complimentary range of washroom products. The response I got was in different. Eddie May fell about laughing when I met him at Cardiff City and promptly told me I didn't have anything big enough to fit him! It was to be a start of a friendship that saw us link up at Torquay a few years later. Having a laugh at Ninnian Park, the next obvious move was to Barnet where on walking into the stand I found the office of a certain Barry Fry. His comments were even more amusing and unfortunately can't be put into print! Swansea were next on the list and after a very successful meeting with Doug Sharp was directed to a Mr Gwillt who led the Commercial Department. It was made plain that if the deal I wanted was to be put into place then they wanted something in return. After a lengthy discussion with John, I went away and came up with a suitable package which was acceptable to both parties. I learnt a lot from that meeting and used the experience to put a foot in the door at other clubs. Two major successes were at Swindon Town and Oxford United. I made many friends at both clubs who are bitter rivals, yet one is a lot more professional than the other. In the past I have supplied over £1, 000 worth of business to Town and £3, 000 to United. Town never pay and even now I am owed £55 for an invoice that is over two years old and I have a delivery note with the Stadium Manager's signature on to prove delivery. Excuses come thick and fast including that Mike Hughes never ordered it, which falls flat on its face having his signature on the delivery note. Despite this I enjoy seeing Andrea Elliott at the club as well as Mike and renewing old friendships with Phil Alexander who was the Commercial Manager before moving to Crystal Palace. My comfort is that Cliff Puffett a Swindon Director's brother Mel does get a lot of business from the club through his business and he struggles to receive payment as well.

Oxford by comparison are a smaller club with cash flow troubles, but they always paid their invoices within 45 days without fail. It is a pleasure doing business with the club and I now look at Gary Whiting the Social Club Secretary as more a personal friend than a business associate.

The package that I really feel happiest about was the one I put together to help Charlton Athletic in their move back to the Valley. This move wiped out any cash they had and even now with their continuing ground improvements find life extremely tough. Numerous meetings with Roy King the Stadium Manager brought success where Mates provided Condom Machines, Ladies Tampon Machines, Air Fresheners etc. The whole of the Valley became a Mates show room. To help extended terms of payment were negotiated and Mates accepted smaller profit margins to give the club and extremely competitive deal. So next time you visit the toilets or offices you can think of me!

The job involved me travelling and staying away the odd night. This I didn't mind too much as I started to fill the evenings out by watching a match instead of sitting in a hotel bedroom. The highlight being Norwich City beating Bayern Munich 4 - 1 in a friendly on 28th January 1992.

Regular meetings with Mike Hughes at Swindon Town were held in the stand as opposed to his office as we discussed prices and products whilst watching the Reserves playing Combination games. The bug was back and my absence from the game concluded.

Having been insulted at Highbury I turned my back on Arsenal after meeting a young Commercial Manager at Charlton called Steve Dixon. He had just taken over from Steve Sutherland who had numerous sponsorship chats with. Through him I found the Addicks were addictive and I had been following the wrong side of my families clubs! Whereas on numerous occasions I had been ignored by the Gunners here was a big club who took an interest in its supporters. This was throughout the club and I often have long chats with Belinda Amiss when I visit the ground, but find Chris Tugwell, John Fuller in fact everyone behind the scenes at Charlton very friendly. Colin Cameron the club's historian then contacted me through Steve to find out more on George Latham. He confirmed the season he played whilst I gave him personal details which should appear in his next book. I have since become a member of the club, a VIP member and most importantly a shareholder.

1991 92 season finished with Teresa begrudgingly letting me out for the odd match. The next season started where the previous one had left off. A visit to Torquay on business was uneventful as the club had delegated the purchasing of my products to a local restaurateur who ran the restaurant in the Boots and Laces club at the ground and owned several tea shops locally. He was happy with his own supplier so disappointed I made my way home via Yeovil where Charlton were playing in a pre season friendly. Most of my friends were not present for the match but Charlton won 3 - 0 so it was compensation for the day's failures. Games followed at Swindon and Bracknell including Town's 5 - 1 win over Notts County before the Big Day! 5th December 1992, one of the most important days in Charlton's recent history. The move back to the Valley for a First Division fixture with Portsmouth. Tickets could have been sold at least three times over but being a VIP member I was entitled to my ticket and took it. Sat in the West Stand next to two former players now in their sixties who were reminiscing on past matches when the East Terrace was crammed full of supporters but now was empty and derelict except for the TV cameras that were present. The pre match entertainment brought past stars onto the pitch including Sailor Brown and Derek Hales and was an emotional event. A lady sat in front of me burst into tears as the teams emerged and walked onto the pitch. She turned round to me and the former players and apologised for sobbing. She had never expected to see the club back at home again in her life! Her comments summed up the whole day and to finish the day off in style the side show to the event - the game, finished with a victory to Charlton 1 - 0 with Colin Walsh carving his name into Charlton Folklaw by scoring the first goal back "Home".

Six weeks later Charlton visited the County Ground and I had my first taste of corporate hospitality in the Directors Box. I entertained my good friend Paul Cook from Apollo Leisure and one of my colleagues from Mates. No mention was made to dress code and whilst Paul and I arrived in Smart Casual attire, Peter arrived in jeans and we were refused admission despite paying £45 each for the tickets. After an argument with a steward we were ushered to our seats and a buffet brought to us in our seats much to the amusement of some of the on looking fans. The club has now a policy of informing visitors as to dress code put into operation after this trip. Swindon rushed into a 2 - 0 lead before Charlton fought back to draw 2 - 2, A satisfactory result. Steve Dixon met me at the game and We agreed to meet up at Twerton Park eleven days later for the Bristol Rovers match. Bath officials got a little mixed up on ticket allocation and whilst Steve and Roy sat in the stand I was put onto the terraces. Winning 2 - 0 was adequate compensation and we met up after the game instead.

My daughter Deborah arrived as did everyone who wanted to see her including Kirstine who called with a dress for her. Christopher was feeling a little put out as he was not getting the attention he was used to. I took him to see his first match when Swindon Reserves took on Portsmouth in the Combination. Having played football on the megadrive all he could keep on asking was
"which team is the computer?"
He lasted 80 minutes before the cold got to him and he asked to go home. Swindon lost the match 3 - 0.

Swindon reached the 1st Division Play Off Final at Wembley and Mel got tickets for a whole bunch of us through his brother Cliff and player David Mitchell. A coach was arranged and I was asked to be at the Shaw Ridge at a time. Teresa took me up to the local Leisure Complex where the team bus was. Beverley Allbright of the club noticed me and said Mel's coach wasn't around frantic driving around followed then I gave up and fortunately having my ticket met up with some Ice Hockey supporters who had a coach going to the game so I went with them arriving at the same time as Mel's coach. It later transpired that he meant the Shaw Ridge behind the Leisure Complex where some of the players lived. It took me a long time to live this down. Half of Swindon were at Wembley claiming to be supporters, Like many other hangers on when clubs reach finals. I wonder where all these supporters have been since they were relegated from the Premier League?

The match proved to be the most exciting in memory for me, having gone 3 - 0 in front and convinced Town had won promotion, having Leicester fight back to 3 - 3 made most of the Swindon's supporters Nervous Wrecks. A shove on Steve White brought a penalty which Paul Bodin converted in the dying minutes to promote Town to the place they were denied a couple of years earlier following the Lou Macari / Brian Hillier scandal at the club.

The return home was a stream of Red scarves despite roadwork's on the M25 holding everyone up for about 45 minutes. Arrival back at Shaw Ridge saw Mel and I climb into Barrie Sandry, the local Golf Professional's car to go and meet the team back at the Devere Hotel were a reception had been organised. Despite an invitation from Cliff I did not attend choosing to go home, whilst Mel went to get changed and join in the celebrations.

The strangest occurrence of the day was later told to me by my best friend Debbie Stayte. She was my daughters Godmother and she was named after her and a friend of both Teresa and I. Up till then I had only met her husband, Andy on one other occasion. He was a dedicated Oxford fan and hated Swindon. He went to Wembley to support Leicester and was not too happy at the result!

Work became strained with a decision from Mate's owners to axe the sales force and continue with a telesales team. Adrian Hughes the

Sales and Marketing Director went along with myself in a long range of cuts. This was after a lot of hard work was put in by all parties to launch the Smiles range of travel kits and toothbrushes. Peter the Crocodile was born and I had my first taste of theatricals! Mates sponsored racing driver Ian McConnell and it was my final job before leaving to take the role over as a crocodile for the product launch. Prancing about in a heavy green costume was great for weight loss and instant recognition for follow up appointments. The best was seeing Paul Cook at Apollo Leisure when I had his secretary announced me at a future appointment

"The crocodile is in reception waiting to see you!"

Next time you are at an airport or railway station and you see a vending machine on the wall, that was me!

Below : Smile Please.

111

Chapter 12
Jolly Hockey Sticks

The very first ice hockey game played at the Link Centre was on July 20th 1985 when Bournemouth Stags played Southampton All Stars. There was a crowd of about 100 who sat in silence and some bewilderment as to what was going on.

Further games were held the following January when Bournemouth switched some of their home league games to Swindon. These tasters generated considerable interest in the game, which was enjoying a national revival after a slump of some 20 years. The visiting players and officials were highly complimentary of the Link Centre facilities, both on and off the ice, and Swindon was finally on the Ice Hockey Map.

It was quickly realised the only way to establish the game in Swindon was to hire the services of an experienced player - coach. An application to the Sports Council for a grant was favourably received and the post of Ice Hockey Development Officer was established.

An appointment was eventually made and an ex - patriot Canadian, Dan Walker, was recruited. A wrangle then followed between the English Ice Hockey Association and the British Ice Hockey Association, the first of many, as to which league Swindon should be admitted to.

The BIHA, seemingly seduced by the Link Centre's exciting facilities, overruled its English counterpart and surprisingly thrust Swindon straight into the National Division One, thus bypassing the usual qualifying leagues. This, though, created a problem, in that there was no skating tradition in Swindon and therefore few ice hockey players of note.

Thamesdown Borough Council, however, with its excellent employment prospects, turned out to be a welcome destination for a small band of mercenary players, many of whom hailed from the depressed North East.

Further grants from the Sport Council supplemented club funds to purchase a consignment of the very expensive equipment required for a team, and the name "Swindon Wildcats" was adopted.

The league was truly a national one which involved three games in Scotland and others in the North East and North West. Despite some misgivings as to the financial viability of the team, they confirmed their membership, and at the eleventh hour a local computer supplies company, Stralfors, stepped in with a sponsorship package that gave some financial security. Stralfors, had a strong association with ice hockey in Sweden, and supported the Wildcats for the next five seasons.

Swindon's first match was on 13th September 1986, but they were on the wrong end of a 15 - 11 scoreline against Altrincham Aces. Their first goal being scored by Dan Walker with assists going to Richie Howe and Daryl Lipsey. For most of the first season the Wildcats struggled to ice a team of any strength, and a general lack of discipline, on and off the ice, left them facing relegation.

Dan Walker suffered a recurrence of an old knee injury while moving house, and was hospitalised for nearly eight weeks. The team Captain, Daryl Lipsey, took charge and a slight change in fortunes left the Wildcats requiring a single point from the last game against high flying Telford Tigers to avoid the drop. That game was probably the one that firmly established ice hockey in Swindon, as a near capacity crowd became emotionally involved in a dramatic and incident-packed cliff hanger. Telford finally won, but ironically, Bournemouth - who had helped so much in the early days - iced an ineligible player in a crucial match, and were deducted two points. Bournemouth were relegated and the cats were down to eight lives.

In 1987, Teresa and I became aware of the club and being only five minutes walk from our house took an interest, but it was to be near the end of the season before we saw our first match.

During the close season, a reappraisal of the entire ice hockey set up was undertaken. It was recognised that some people were good at organising ice hockey and some were good at organising, but a combination of both was highly improbable. As a result, the administrative, financial and promotional aspects of ice hockey were clearly defined as Link Centre Management Functions, with the ice hockey development officer providing the ice expertise.

It was clearly recognised that the way forward was for the creation of a junior development programme to encourage local talent and to produce home grown players for the future. The new ice hockey development officer, Daryl Lipsey, was a popular choice and undertook this objective. To his credit Daryl's junior development project has been a success with many of the juniors breaking into the senior squad over the past two seasons.

The 1987-88 season got underway, but the cats were still frustrated by not being able to secure the services of sufficient good players. however, a more settled team was frequently on the brink of surprise victories over some of the top teams, only to naively let the opponents slip, through inexperience.

The local support continued to grow as the crowd came to appreciate the nature of the sport and identified it as exciting and good value entertainment, in safe and comfortable surroundings. The Link Centre's marketing efforts concentrated on these factors and, despite indifferent results on the ice, attendance's increased to double those of the first season.

Teresa and I now well aware of the publicity ventured down to see our first match against Southampton Vikings on 5th March 1988. TV cameras were making a rare visit to cover the game and highlights and an interview with Daryl Lipsey was shown on BBC West and consequently screened before the next home match at the Link Centre on the screens opposite the main stand. The Wildcats won an entertaining match 11 - 8 and I was hooked going to as many games as I could. Even Teresa enjoyed the game and came along to matches with me until Christopher was born. After that she lost interest and although still goes it is now only a few games a season.

The following day we both visited my parents who live about half a mile from the John Nike Leisure Complex in Bracknell and saw a

2nd Division match between the Bracknell Bees and the Peterborough Titans, which Peterborough won 12 - 6. The Wildcats followed their success over Southampton, by beating the Richmond Flyers 10 - 3. Teresa's only ever away match followed on 20th March when we took the supporters coach to Gillingham to see a loss to the Medway Bears 11 - 5. The coach driver decided to take a different route and got lost in London. We missed most of the first period and I lost confidence in the supporters club. I approached Daryl Lipsey to offer my help and made a very close friend whom I rate as one of my best friends.

Daryl is a Canadian who was born in 1963 in North Battleford, Saskatchewan. A great sportsman who enjoyed golf, baseball and water-skiing and during his single days cooking. A year after the Heineken 1st Division was formed he moved to England and became one of Bournemouth Stags "Import" players. During which time he clocked up 200 points and was awarded the honour of Best Import (1984) and most Popular Player (1984 and 1985). He moved to Swindon for the sides first year of Ice Hockey and after taking over the development officer post from Dan Walker continued to improve the youngsters until he was offered a large increase in his salary to move to the newly formed giants Manchester Storm. He was the first player to score 1000 1st Division points and after receiving his Dual National passport, was the first player to represent the Wildcats as a Great Britain International. He married Alison in 1992 and Teresa and I were privileged to be invited to the Wedding. To cement the close ties I have always had with him he became Christopher's Godfather and even delayed leaving for a match so he and Alison could attend Deborah's christening. He proved how good a friend he was following the break up of my marriage. In a busy three weeks both he and Alison were rushing around wondering what was going on within the Ice Hockey club. That period saw my neighbour Alison's husband run off back to America, two sets of parents of young players in the team swap partners, Teresa leave to go to another neighbour and finally Sue Aldridge whom I still see at the club finding out her husband Arthur was seeing someone else in my road behind her back. Freshbrook quickly became the hot bed of romance and intrigue! Daryl stood by me and took me under his wing giving me morale support from a man's point of view. The comfort factor came from my two closest friends Debbie Stayte and Caryn Puffett. Between them all I doubt if I would have got through it all!

I obtained sponsorship for the team and spent my 23rd birthday watching the Swindon (Reserve side) Cougars play against Hastings Monarchs. After the game Daryl presented me with an ice hockey puck which was the very first of a sponsorship package on sponsoring the match puck that still exists at the club to this day!

I was to see 9 matches this season, the fewest games I was ever to attend in a season. Two of which were to be sponsored Cougars matches. The cougars included my former Wokingham team mate Paul Mitchell which gave me added reason to lend my support. The team actually finished as runners - up in their league in their first ever season, a feat that was mostly down to Daryl's development programme.

1988-89 season saw more signings with Kel Land the popular re classified Import joining from Telford Tigers. But the highlight of the season was in front of a full house and an electric atmosphere, the Wildcats pulled off a sensational 13 - 8 victory on November 19th against the Cardiff Devils, to become one of only two sides to defeat the Division One Champions. I got to see most of the home games including a match between Austria and Korea in Pool C of the Under 21 World Championships which was staged at the Link Centre.

1989-90 brought a new Import in the shape of Scott Koberinski and his enthusiastic wife Debbie. Scott became a good friend and other than Daryl the only other player I really befriended. I tended to keep the players at distance fearing I may be viewed as another hanger on which is probably why both Daryl and Scott appreciated my company. I suffered two clashes over two other imports Shane MacEachern and Pat Ford during the season after Daryl had asked for some help in providing items to help them settle in. Crockery and cutlery were some items that Teresa and I gave them to assist their moving in. They both quit the club after a few weeks to return back to North America taking everything including my bits and pieces with them. I've been a bit wary ever since and although current players Bryan Larkin and Gary Dickie have known me for a while now and will always stop to chat when they see me, I tend to give them their privacy. However, since Bryan married Natasha, a local skating professional and the birth of their daughter Isabella, we have spoken more often as both devoted parents we now have more in common. He is one of eight children and can't work out how his parents coped. All I could say was

"Wait till you have a second and they are both fighting regularly!"

The most amusing match was a Charity match organised between Daryl and local Speedway rider Alan Rossiter. John Lawless at Cardiff also joined in. What followed was classed as a Swindon Select against a Cardiff Select, but in reality it was half Ice Hockey players and Speedway riders trying to stay on their feet. The final result was deemed 14 - 13 to the Swindon side, but with about 25 players on the ice for a free for all it was hard to tell what was going on! The real winners though were the charities who benefited from the games proceeds. The event was recreated in 1996 and proved to be just as successful and the speedway riders had by now learnt to skate - just! Sky TV even turned up to film highlights thus promoting the two sports in Swindon which receive little publicity on TV these days.

1990 - 91 saw Debbie Koberinski turn up the volume on her cheers and everyone knew where she was at the rink, this is only partly matched today by one of the player's mothers who sits not too far away from me in Block B. Debbie was a typical American who rallied all the other players wives and girlfriends together and formed a sort of cheerleader group. When she and Scott returned back to the States they were sorely missed. I kept in touch with him for a while through Daryl, and he was one of the most popular players to play in Swindon along with Kel Land and Daryl himself. The team itself improved on past seasons by actually reaching the play offs but failed at the final hurdle losing 10 - 11 in a close battle with the arch enemy Slough Jets.

117

1991 - 92 will always be remembered with affection as arguably the year that the Cats finally left their mark on Ice Hockey and someone's face! Scott returned for his third year and was joined by Bryan Larkin and Ryan Stewart who became known as Malcolm the Mountie in parts of the Link for his ambition to join up. He in fact left to do that and is rumoured to be returning to play in this country again in 1997 with another club! Daryl now having his dual National passport became a non import and such was the league rules at the time, Kel was not allowed to stay and play as the team were restricted to one dual national only. Kel joined Solihull before they had cash troubles when he moved to Scotland to play for the Fife Flyers. Because of his love for Swindon and his popularity he was always given a standing ovation from the fans when his teams provided the opposition at the Link Centre.

The season provided the first ever "Shut Out" by a netminder at Swindon, when Blackburn were defeated 20 - 0 on 18th January, but the Cats finest hour was arguably on 23rd November at the newly opened Sheffield Ice Arena. When the Wildcats reached the final of the Autumn Trophy and were drawn to face the up and coming Milton Keynes Kings. After going 4 - 0 down they fought back to tie the game at 5 - 5. Overtime failed to separate the teams and a sudden death penalty shoot-out occurred which Swindon just won 8 - 7. I have never felt as much tension as I did that night! One person who will remember the evening for the rest of his life is my near neighbour Alan Emery. He was sat two rows in front of me and only got to see the first ten minutes of Kings dominance. In a moment of panic Daryl had flipped the ice hockey puck in the air and out of the rink. It promptly hit Alan in the face knocking some of his teeth out. The puck is made of solid vulcanised rubber and frequently travels at speeds over 100 miles per hour depending on who has hit it. So beware it can be a dangerous sport to watch if you don't keep your eye on the game! Alan returned from hospital to see the penalty shoot out. Daryl has always felt guilty about the incident as he has been friends with Alan ever since he first moved to Swindon and lodged with his neighbour Bob Radford.

Mickey Stafford who was never the most placid of players was then banned from the sport for deliberately attempting to injure an official after receiving a gross misconduct penalty at Blackburn. Then Swindon again reached the play offs and defeated Basingstoke 7 - 6, but just missed out on promotion. That was a year to remember!

1992 - 93 Tragedy was to strike when Director Mike Bishop and father of player, Alan died of a heart attack, but on a lighter side saw Scott become a father on February 8th, with the birth of a 8 LB 5 oz daughter who was named Taylor Shea Koberinski. Debbie wanted to raise her in America so Scott was never to return to play for the Cats again. The largest scoreline ever recorded at the Link Centre then followed with a crushing 32 - 0 victory over the Wightlink Raiders, who started the final period by singing "Always look on the Bright Side of Life". Their attitude throughout was a credit to the sport and it was recognised by the reception they received when they left the ice. Milton Keynes Kings gained revenge for Sheffield by knocking the Cats out of the Trophy at the Semi Final stage, but Swindon responded by beating the massive Sheffield Steelers 9 - 8 and reaching the play offs again.

The following season was a slight disappointment, but finished on a high. I was by now sponsoring Neil Browne and was happy to travel to Oxford for the Final League game of the season and not only provide the City Stars with their record defeat of 21 - 4, but Neil claimed enough points to overhaul Steve Nell's record of Top British points scorer in a season with 119 points.

1994 -95 Saw a successful season with the team again doing well to reach the play offs but again falling at the last hurdle and just missing out despite beating Premier League side Whitley Warriors at the Link Centre 10 - 4. My kids had taken an interest in the sport by this time and Christopher attended his first match on 18th March to see
a narrow 11 - 10 loss to the Slough Jets again. He loved it and went to the Whitley game with me also.

On 19th February 1995, Sky TV in the guise of The Discovery Channel paid a visit to the Link Centre to film a documentary about

Ice Hockey and its players. They chose to film Lee Valley Lions losing 15 - 2 to Swindon. I am on it, but blink and you'll miss me. Keith Pike is more than visable sitting in front of me with his red jacket on, but the camera crew were busy interviewing and filming the Lee Valley supporters directly below us. Lee Valley Lions had a second session in front of the cameras a few weeks later being chosen to feature in cold remedy adverts for SmithKline Beecham which are still being shown on TV. Of the officials on that day all three are known to me. Chris Borg being a former player for Swindon in their first season, but now concentrating on being a linesman. The other Linesman, Mark Thompson lives a few doors away from Debbie with his parents Keith and Sue whom I sit near each week. He also edits the girls ice hockey programme when not a college as sister Louise plays for the Topcats. As to the referee. Jamie Crapper, I knew him well as an import player for the Bracknell Bees then again when he moved to John Nike's other ice Rink in Bristol to be the complexes Manager. He took up refereeing but in my opinion is not as competent as when he was a player! He got so much stick from supporters over his surname, that he changed it to Craipper.

1995 saw the emergence of the Manchester Storm and the Nynex arena - the largest of its type in Europe. John Lawless had moved from Cardiff to manage the side and took Daryl with him as his assistant. It broke Daryl's heart to leave the cats, but he had differing views with the Wildcats supremo Bill Roache, so evaluated his
career and having past his prime accepted the challenge and the increased salary offer to move up to Lancashire. A move I could understand and totally accept. Unfortunately some didn't see it that way and he received boos from some ungrateful fans who had forgotten all that he had done for the team over the years, when he returned with the Storm for a league fixture. Swindon surprisingly won 10 - 6, and end Manchester's record breaking run and 100% away record. With both Christopher and Deborah in attendance to see their "uncle" Daryl play. What the fans failed to realise was that he had come down the previous night and spent the evening with

Alison's parents. Duties then done, had spent the whole day at the rink watching the juniors playing and giving encouragement to the kids he had taught for the past few years. I had arranged with him to meet him prior to the Ladies Ice Hockey team match and Christopher then sat with his godfather whilst watching my next door neighbour Michelle Groundwater playing for the Swindon Topcats and losing 5 - 1 to Telford. I enjoy watching the girls playing hockey not only so I can support Michelle but to also watch Debbie Hinder who is also becoming a very close friend to me!

The Storm game was also marked by the making of two more friends, Tony and Mandy Dickinson. Tony is a Director of the club and both he and Mandy have been through similar personal backgrounds, so it became very easy to bond with them. The first time I really got talking to them was the following evening at Telford Ice Rink when Mandy grabbed me as I left the Gents toilet, as she was looking for her husband who happened to also be in the loos. I do tend to remember the strangest of details!

The Nynex arena was completed in August and I accepted an invitation to have a nose round the place before it opened, work commitments caused a slight postponement by a couple of weeks and I had the tour prior to a Take That concert. We stopped to watch the band rehearse before viewing the rest of the facilities. I did not think too highly of the group who then had both Daryl and I thrown out of Daryl's own office so they could prepare for the concert doors opening a few minutes later. I returned with some of my friends, Sue Aldridge, the Richardson's and the Davie's for the first ever Home match a 6 - 6 tie with Telford Tigers. While most of the coach load went shopping in the Arndale Centre I spent time with Bob Radford, Alan Emery and Daryl in his office. When Daryl gave the others a tour I left to find Dave Richardson on Daryl's instructions as he had been given some bad news about David's father. I eventually found him and informed him. His dad later died in hospital so will not forget his first visit to the Nynex Arena in a hurry!

Apart from the Altrincham Aces, Ice Hockey was a new sport in the

City, even a Steward asked me how many periods their were such was the newness of the whole arena and staff not to mention the crowd of bewildered onlookers. Keen to promote the sport Allsports had agreed to be the sponsors and replica shirts were available in the shop. To promote the shirts Daryl gave me a little inside information as to the location of these shirts and with a bit of promoting from the Ogden Ice Hockey Ltd, the owners of the rink, I wandered around the concourse prior to the gates opening with a Storm replica shirt on. The owners loved it and I kept the shirt, thus becoming the first non player to ever wear a Manchester Storm shirt!

The atmosphere and presentation at the arena is second to none and a credit to the sport. A pity that the organisers treat fans like football hooligans though. Initially as the sport was growing I encountered no trouble and visited the rink several times to see Daryl. The last visit on 11th February 1996, though will probably be my last by coach because of the treatment we had received. Past visits were finished off in the pub opposite the arena having drinks with the players. However, Solihull supporters had caused a few problems a few weeks previously and we were then treated with the same brush. We had to sit in one area to avoid trouble, then found Storm supporters buying the spare seats were we were sitting making a mockery of the ticket allocation. Then the final insult was after the match, not only were we held back until all the Storm fans had left the building, but were then herded like sheep into the awaiting coach and sent home. We were refused access to the pub by arena officials despite having the permission of the players and the pub had nothing to do with the arena what so ever. This got a little too much for our placid group and Jaynie Davies had to be restrained. The actions of incompetent officials nearly caused the trouble that they were trying to avoid. Most on the coach committed to make this their last visit not because of the game which we lost, but because of the heavy handiness of stewards. Ice Hockey is a family sport with little trouble at matches unless it is Solihull supporters who tend to be unruly, but their actions seem to be spoiling the sport which is really starting to boom over the past two seasons.

Swindon reorganised for the 1996 season and a change of owner helped after Jaynie and numerous others staged demonstrations to save the sport in the town. As Bill Roche owned the name Wildcats, the team changed to the Icelords and broke most of their old club records in a very successful season which is still going on as I write.

However, the season was also to contain an unnecessary incident when just prior to Christmas, Swindon as league leaders travelled to second placed Solihull for a league fixture and in a tense game Solihull's Steve Carpenter caused a serious injury to Gary Dickie. The result was a premature end to Gary's playing career. Legal action is now planned by the club against Solihull for the lack of Safety personnel on duty and a personal law suit is also in the pipeline against Steve. The league fixture computer then put the two sides against each other twice in the space of a few weeks. The result was a bad tempered affair which resulted in a mass brawl at the Link Centre with 2 seconds remaining on the clock and four players sent from the ice for fighting.

The world of Ice Hockey was shocked at the extent of Gary's injuries and a testimonial was quickly organised when an All Star side beat Swindon 11 - 10 on 22nd January and approximately £10, 000 was raised for my friend.

Whilst I view football as my second profession, Ice Hockey is how I relax. For 10 years I have sat in virtually the same seat in block B and made many friends as the fans come back year after year. The lovely Mandy sits with her family a few seats to my left, Keith and Sonia directly in front and Shaun to my right with his dad. Sue, Sandra and Keith normally sit around my area and Shaun's ex girlfriend Jenny sits a few rows behind. I know most of our local area in the block and the only disruption occurs when Christopher and Deborah want to come along for a game. I have to be careful with them though as they are in their talkative stage, Christopher being 7 and Deborah 4. Shaun is also the name of Christopher's hamster and he nearly called Shaun (the person) a hamster earlier in the season, whilst Deborah embarrassed a fan who was sitting behind me by constantly

123

talking about her artificial hand, that she wanted one and could she buy one from the club shop? We are a happy band of friends drawn together by the love of the sport and Ice Hockey is a much more friendly, family orientated sport than football. I am well known for being either quiet at matches or daft as a brush! Christmas 1996 was no different as I attended the last home game before Christmas against Slough Jets on the 12th December wearing my Santa hat with "Santa is a Swindon Supporter" written on it, which I got from the County Ground the previous year. The word "Wally" was mentioned by more than one party pooper. Only Sue Aldridge had joined in wearing a pair of antlers. The others were dressed as normal and completely disowning me. You can't be boring or miserable otherwise people avoid you. I know as I've found to my cost. I have suffered more than most in my life, but try to put up a curtain of happiness to remain popular. Only those very close to me can see the cracks in my armour!

I could write more on the sport but this chapter would become a book within a book, so watch out for a possible sequel one day!

Chapter 13
Bowled Over by Beefy

1993 saw a lot more changes in my life! My business was doing reasonably well until I ran into a few problems with Directors and a large company going into receivership owing my company over £10, 000. The annoying thing was they reset up again 24 hours later with the directors wives taking over as directors and maintaining the same contracts so overnight they wrote off all their debts and no one could do anything about it. That plus a few other contracts which failed to pay up what was promised and the wake of a failed marriage with debts and solicitors bills cost me personally approximately £45, 000 over a three year period. My parents remortaged their house to half the debt to relieve some of the pressure on me, but as my dad is 55 the building society would not let him borrow anymore than he could afford to pay back over a 10 year period. Whilst I feel guilty at them doing that, without their help I would have followed my former father in law to bankruptcy. The debt is still high but I am working to reduce it frustrated by our common laws who allow events as described to exist as everyday occurrences.

My Cricket career started and ended in May. a year later when I had a trial with Gloucestershire, who said I wasn't good enough, but I enjoyed the experience. I was then invited to the families day when the kids enjoyed bowling at the players and had a chance to meet my friends Chris Broad and Jack Russell.

My first visit to the County Ground in Bristol was as a result of an appointment with Philip August the Chief Executive who I had chased for a few months on the subject of sanitary bins. I had a dummy bin as a result of a request from Richard Stevens the buyer at Wadworth's Brewery in Devizes, who had asked me to go round every single ladies toilet in every managed house that they owned and provide a recommendation as to how many were on each site and if further bins were required and would they fit in the cubicles. Armed with a bin I then visited every pub, this was okay until I reached the end of the tour in Southampton. After knocking and hearing no reply I entered the last loos of the trip and all was quiet. I flung open the toilet doors to see an old lady sat on the toilet in mid stream with a very pitiful look on her face. I don't know who was more embarrassed her or me! After the event I had kept hold of the offending item and Philip had requested to see it as it was taller and narrower than other standard bins. I was summoned to appear on Thursday 20th May 1993. In theory Gloucestershire were to have played Durham in the county championships and it was raining heavily so no play had started. I walked through the club and passed Ian Botham who was chatting to Wayne Larkins, something was said which I didn't hear but guessed it concerned me walking around with a sanitary bin under my arm. Ian then took it from me an briefly tried to use it as a cricket bat much to the amusement of the onlookers by the restaurant. I had my meeting and returned to the club as a member a few days later at the request of Jack Russell. Jack as I'm sure you are aware is a very talented artist and has an excellent agent called Jim Rushton who promotes his paintings. Jim is also a good photographer but was not at the game and what was to be Ian's last match at Bristol before retiring was Jack's last chance to realise a lifetime's ambition to get Ian out. He did so by stumping him. I had my SLR available and took some shots. Fortunately I took two of the event, the only person in the whole ground who captured the historic moment on film. Jack was over joyed and I later received a print of Ian Botham that Jack had drawn with an inscription on it which read "To Stuart, to commemorate Botham, Stumped Russell, Bowled Davies, 73, 24th May 1993" and signed. It is now framed with the photo and hanging in my living room!

I split from Teresa a few weeks into the football season and refound the game as it became a way with Ice Hockey to forget my personal problems. It is amazing though that when couples split some friends are lost. Fortunately I retained most of them but was looked on differently. As a couple no problem, but now as a single male the

126

husbands became a little uncertain in case I proved a threat to their marriages. Whilst Mel Puffett went one way and constantly joked as he begged me to take his wife Caryn off his hands, others at the other end of the scale were nervous in case I did!

The season opened with a short trip down the road to see Salisbury City lose 2 - 1 to Charlton Athletic then a return to Anvil Lane. Whilst driving round the M25 on 29th July, I tuned into Capital Radio to hear Mick Brown announce that Cobham were playing hosts to Millwall in a benefit match for the late Eddie Davis. This came as a shock as I knew Eddie very well when he assisted the committee a few season's earlier. I promptly turned the car around and headed for the club. Chris Bird, the physio was on sentry duty to ensure everyone paid to watch the match and we spent most of the evening chatting over what had happened since my previous visit. A Millwall Director arrived and refused to pay instead giving me his business card which proved he was a director. Keith Stevens, who plays for Millwall and is an old friend of both myself and the club was shocked to hear about how tight his director was when the subject was mentioned after the final whistle. Millwall won 4 - 0 with John Byrne scoring a hat trick.

Wokingham played Southampton and I had my first chance to see a young player who could have a very successful career in front of him. Paul Sherrin who joined from my old side Alloa Athletic, even my dad ventured out to his annual match for this one. Saints won 2 - 0. I renewed old friendships with Roy Merryweather's son Kevin who had played in the same side as me what now seemed like years ago. He was now not only working behind the bar at the club, but was player manager of the Reserve side.

Then onto the Premiership. Swindon's match with Liverpool in front of the live Sky cameras. I had to make do with a place in the Town End which I hated as I could not see the Stratton Bank end very clearly, even with my glasses on. The result was a predictable 5 - 0 win to the Merseysiders. The game with Manchester City was not much better with Swindon taking the lead through a Nicky Summerbee free kick only to have Niall Quinn cancel out the effort and then City scored two further goals one of which was "miles" offside in the dying minutes. I could predict even then that this was going to be a short stay in the Premiership for Swindon!

Bore all was the result of a trip to Ashton Gate. Sat with Steve Dixon, Roy King and John Fuller in the officials area proved little satisfaction as both Bristol City and Charlton failed to excite and a 0 - 0 stalemate was reached.

Above: Christopher with my good friend Jack Russell
Below: With Les Robinson (Oxford United) and my "other family"
Rachel, Debbie and Andy Stayte.

The first trip to Plainmoor was a must. I had taken a holiday in Goodrington Sands the previous season with my family and was refused to be allowed to go by Teresa who put her foot down firmly. Having been at the ground many times for business my first match didn't come until 27th October when the reserves were in action and defeated Exeter City 2 - 1. My company had enough business for a couple of days in the region, so I stayed with my friend Mike Morgan, who owns three hotels in the region. It made a change to be away from my troubles! To ease the situation over the separation I had vacated the marital home for a couple of months to allow some breathing space for decisions between Teresa and I. I moved back to Wokingham to live with my parents. This was not ideal as they had got used to their own company and space, so my presence was a bit of a strain at times for us all. However, although I had my disagreements with both my parents over the years, this chapter in my life pulled us together and made us much closer and I am now proud to have my parents.

Driving up the motorway every weekend to see my children was a drain on me emotionally as Teresa barred me from the house and I had no where to go other than round to Caryn and Mel's or Debbie's, failing that an hours drive back to Wokingham which meant four hours in the car every day just to keep both my children amused. One such weekend was on the 30th October, having just driven back from Wokingham with both Christopher and Deborah asleep on the back seat, I pulled up in the County Ground car park and wound the window down. The local radio station had live commentary of the game with Aston Villa on and I could hear the crowd noises and so spent the second half of the match contemplating what a mess I was in. The fact Swindon lost 2 - 1 didn't seem to bother me I was too tired and depressed to notice. I hardly slept for three months, was highly stressed out and hit the bottle to drown my sorrows. Suicide was a pleasing option which crossed my mind on more than one occasion, thankfully Debbie talked me to my senses! The lowest point was still to come as my body decided enough was enough and after talking on the phone at Oxford Services went back to the car and blacked out. The shock triggered my emotions and with both Caryn's and Debbie's continuous support I got through it.

A trip to Selhurst Park to see Wimbledon beat Swindon 3 - 0, then a peaceful visit to the Valley for Charlton's 5 - 1 victory over Notts County calmed me down. Shaun Newton's splendid goal from outside the box giving me the most cheer. Two more trips to Devon in the following couple of weeks help me to clear my mind and walking along the Torquay seafront even in cold December made me start thinking of the positive sides of my life. - The kids who adored me and my friends and Parents who thought so much of me that they devoted most of their time to ensuring I was all right. I gave myself a reason to live. Watching Torquay's Reserve team defeat Bournemouth 3 - 0 put the icing on the cake. People sometimes look at me as if I am daft having such a close tie with the struggling 3rd Division club. They didn't know quite how badly I was suffering and that the club albeit unknowingly helped pull me back together again. I am a loyal individual at heart and close ties are very hard to break with me, that is why Torquay, Caryn and Debbie have a very special place in my life!

Teresa moved out into rented accommodation with her boyfriend until his wife had vacated his house and I moved back into a by now emptied marital home on Christmas Eve. I renamed the house "Fork Hall" on re-entering it. As part of the divorce anything that was worth anything went to Teresa or was split between us. The house however, was in negative equity and she was not prepared to pay me half the difference of the debt so I had the house. This may be the only time I've every been glad of the slump in the property market. People ask me why It was named Fork Hall, but all laugh when I tell them "Because that is exactly what it is worth!"

A few days before, my parents had sent me to Adams Park to see Wycombe's new ground and their 2 - 0 3rd Division victory over Carlisle as the club was nearby. Having spent Christmas Day on my own with the exception of a brief visit from Teresa to collect the kids presents I sat down in a by now nearly completely furnished house as a result of a very hectic day of purchasing the previous afternoon, I ate some cold turkey my mother had cooked for me before I had moved out, and bawled my eyes out! This was the worst Christmas I had ever had and I was all alone. All my friends had their own commitments with their own relatives and I didn't want to burden them or ruin their special day, so I opened a bottle of brandy and polished it off rather quickly. I never want to go through those months and a Christmas like that again! Boxing Day I collected the kids and took them to Wokingham for the traditional family gathering. Having to drive them back again that evening was probably the best thing I did as it meant I didn't drink. It wouldn't have taken much for me to become an alcoholic and the day without booze went a long way to drying me out and preparing myself for the long road to recovery.

Mel persuaded me to go to see Chelsea play at Swindon on New Year's day. He was a season ticket holder in the North Stand, but the stand had sold out. I got into the Stratton Bank but could only see the crossbar at that end of the ground because of the amount of supporters heads that were in front of me. Glenn Hoddle's return and a victory to the blues 3 - 1. Now firmly under Mel's wing we both go to the games together and I have hardly missed a match at the ground since!

Charlton Athletic again beckoned and as I had to collect some items of clothing left behind in Wokingham tied the two together and after seeing the Addicks win 2 - 1 against West Bromwich Albion returned to my parents house and spent the night there. My new life was starting to take shape again slowly. Ipswich drew 1 - 1 in the FA Cup 3rd Round before Jason decided he wanted to come down with his family to see his beloved Spurs side play. I queued for nearly two hours to get the four seats together and took some comfort that it was not wasted as Jason got quite upset when Town actually won the game 2 - 1. A winning streak they extended by beating Coventry 3 - 1 the following match. I then decided to purchase a season ticket for all the remaining matches and was promptly refused by the club's ticket office. The reason they gave was because they had yet to play

Manchester United at home and felt most fans would buy just for that match. I could never see the logic in that comment as even if a supporter had done that for the one match, with 7 matches left to play the club would have the money for 7 tickets either way. Politics within the club meant I lost my battle and had to continue to queue with everyone else two weeks prior to the match when the tickets were issued. The club certainly know how to get my back up! The queue for the Manchester United game took me closer to three hours to get two tickets, one for me and one for a friend of Mel's. Having the ticket stubs to prove I was a regular. Being issued with the season ticket when I asked would have avoided a lot of queuing on my part and a lot of administrative costs for the club. One day they will learn the art of good public relations and marketing!

Debbie's husband Andy then came on the scene and I started going to matches with him from time to time. Our first match together was particularly memorable as Oxford were on their way to being relegated and the match I attended was against Charlton. We easily won 4 - 0 and Andy was so uptight given Oxford's league position he got up with ten minutes to go and walked out. I met up with him in the players lounge afterwards with a big grin on my face and dispite going to see the 1 - 1 draw with West Bromwich Albion with him, was branded a jinx and banned from going to the last game of the season. Oxford won that game but were relegated anyway so it would not have made much of a difference had I gone. Andy is very dedicated to Oxford and even has lucky studs which he wears in his pierced ears for special matches. He taught me just what addiction to football was all about! His friends especially Lisa frowned on me to start with knowing I went to "Scum" as they referred to Swindon Town, but I was tolerated for about 12 months but after seeing me on a regular basis now I am accepted.

After a Saturday match most of Andy's crowd go pubbing and I joined them after the Charlton match, when they took the train to Reading. This was the biggest boozing session I can remember and apparently this happens as a regular occurrence with them. I can't keep up with the amount consumed and begrudge spending the cash on that amount, so I hardly go on a Saturday, but will attend most midweek games when a pint before and after the game is acceptable.

A customer invited me to see Plymouth Argyle's match with Blackpool in February, other than seeing the Pilgrims win 2 - 1, I went along to the game as it was a "new ground" for me and helped push me nearer to my target of seeing a match at all 92 League grounds in England. Some would argue that it is 93 as Berwick Rangers who play in the Scottish League are in England, but then again the 92 include clubs in Wales and Chester's new stadium which is situated on the border. One half being in England, but cross the pitch to the other side of the ground and you find yourself in Wales! To counter the argument over Berwick I visited the ground whilst with Alloa so at least I don't have to go to that place again!

My highlight of the season was my first visit to Old Trafford to see Charlton's 3 - 1 FA Cup Quarter Final defeat. I may hate the club, but no one can dislike the ground or its facilities which I found better than Wembley Stadium and the goods on sales just as extorsionate. The following week was Manchester United again for their 2 - 2 draw at Scum (sorry Swindon Andy seems to be having some influence). The game was probably best remembered for the sending off of Eric Cantona for stamping on John Moncur. Having been sat about 10 feet from the incident I can vouch for the severity of the assault!

Sky paid one of their brief visits to a non Manchester game for the visit of Sheffield Wednesday. Never have I felt so robbed of a point as I did that night. I think it was Kevin Watson who got the winner but Swindon had to suffer an injury to Fraser Digby, the goalkeeper that the referee let go. So allowing Kevin to slot home to an open goal whilst Frazer was lying on the ground in pain. A position he was in for over 30 seconds previous to the goal being scored.

A 0 - 0 to Bury proved to be an unsatisfactory final visit of the season to Torquay, but Swindon's 4 - 2 defeat with Wimbledon made up for the lack of goals in Torbay. The league season finished with the visit of Leeds United to the County Ground. As a gesture of thanks towards Andy for the support both he and Debbie had given me I treated him to a ticket in the Directors box for Swindon's final game in the Premiership. Swindon needed to avoid conceding five goals in the match, otherwise they would have been relegated having conceded a record 100 goals in the league that season. Much to Andy's delight Leeds scored number five of their 5 - 0 victory deep into injury time. He could not contain his delight as he leaped in the air with his arms raised. He jumped so high and at an angle he nearly jumped out of the Directors Box!

My season had not quite finished as an invitation arrived to go to Wembley for the Evening Standard 5 A Side tournament. I had never been to one but seen them on TV so was fascinated and grabbed the ticket willingly. I had not been let down either it was one of the best seats in the house three rows from the front in the executive area. Any one who tuned into Sky Sports that evening would have been sick of seeing me in the background shots most of the time! The area was reserved for players guests and I sat next to a couple who said their son played for West Ham. They disappeared part of the way though the tournament and then a voice came from the seat asking if he could look at the programme. It was Harry Redknapp the West Ham manager. I had been given a free ticket in the West Ham section. I spent about half an hour with Harry chatting over some of the games he had earlier missed and found him to be extremely polite and courteous, which is more than could be said for Wimbledon owner Sam Hamman. He kept insisting on standing directly in front of our group and refusing to move. he was arrogant and rude to the stadium officials when they asked him to move. Vinney Jones was managing the Wimbledon side that evening and managed to persuade Sam to move along a little to avoid an incident. Despite his hard man reputation it became quite obvious to those sat around me that evening that off the pitch he is in fact quite a gentle and likeable person. When Harry moved off to sort out his West Ham youngsters something was said to the main organiser about Sam and within 10 minutes the event organiser was with us apologising about Sam and saying he was unable to do anything about it. Tony Adams then joined in and brought the European Cup Winners Cup with him that Arsenal had just won, which he was about to go onto the pitch with to show the crowd. He sat in Harry's seat and gave me the cup to pass around the group for a few minutes. It certainly made the evening memorable for me. But it had yet to finish! Some light hearted rivalry had broken out between Wycombe Wanderers who were playing in their first ever London 5 a side tournament and West Ham as all the players guests were close by. Wycombe then beat the Hammers 1 0 in the Semi final to meet Wimbledon in the final. Now this was like a red rag to a bull seeing Sam emerge again, so both the Wycombe and West Ham crowd jeered Wimbledon and cheered the underdogs who after drawing 0 - 0 took the final to penalties. The Moroccan keeper Chuck Mousadik then displayed heroics as Wycombe won the shoot out 1 - 0. A very overjoyed group of officials then started to cheer and get over excited. The next few minutes were a bit of a blur as they went berserk celebrating and Martin O Neill who was by now standing next to me gave me two complimentary tickets for Wycombe's play off home tie with Carlisle United. These tickets included a full three course meal in the restaurant and a tour of the ground including the dressing rooms. I was happy to accept this gift and took Andy along as it was a new ground for him. The meal was excellent but we were distracted after receiving a call on my mobile phone from Debbie's friend Caroline informing us that Debbie had taken her daughter Rachel to hospital following a fall. Caroline proved to be a little mellow dramatic as the wound was not that serious and had us both worried over nothing. Wycombe won the match 2 - 1 and reached the Final on a 4 - 1 aggregate victory and promotion to the 2nd Division, via an exciting Final at Wembley.

So ended probably the most dramatic season of my life!

Chapter 14
A New Beginning

My work was now moving me around the country and a chance conversation with Dennis Smith at Oxford United made me look at football at a different angle! I passed him whilst on a business trip to the club and we stopped for a chat. I told him I was moving around a lot and watching matches whilst away as it was better than watching TV in a hotel bedroom. He then said:

"If you see anyone worthwhile let me know".

I had never thought of scouting as a profession but it seemed like a good idea to use my experiences in that capacity. I decided that I had my season ticket for Swindon and got up to Oxford whenever I could, but that still left a lot of spare time as the Football League always seem to have both Swindon and Oxford playing at home on the same Saturdays. My spare time could be used in a capacity that I would enjoy rather than vegetate at home in front of the TV or in a pub somewhere. And so "The Scout" was born!

First stop was down on the Torbay coast for Torquay's friendly with Middlesbrough. It was Bryan Robson's first game in charge and not only did he play, but he scored a good goal as well in his side's 2 - 0 victory over my adopted club.

With my kids away on holiday with their mother and step father I used the time to my advantage and saw 4 matches in 4 consecutive days. Simon Barker was on trial at Swindon having fallen out with the management at Queens Park Rangers. Having just been relegated from the Premiership Swindon were anxious to try out their whole squads at matches so I travelled up to Gloucester City for their friendly. Sure enough the game was played by two Swindon teams, the first team took the first half and the rest made up the team for the second half. Being a local derby on a warm day with a carnival being staged outside the ground a large crowd was expected and received. Gloucester City lost 3 - 1 which included a spectacular goal from my friend Ross MacLaren with a lob from near the half way line. He told me a couple of seasons later that it was his last goal and gave him a lot of satisfaction! The following evening Highworth Town were officially opening their floodlights with a match against QPR. To start with The Swindon Ladies team played a friendly. I was surprised to see a few faces I recognised in the team. The Queens Park Rangers side was almost full strength including Dichio and Sinclair. They comfortably won 4 - 0 but the crowd probably made it Highworth's record for receipts as a marquee was provided for additional beer sales as it was another warm evening and most of the spectators took full advantage of abusing the FA rule of being in sight of a match whilst drinking alcohol.

Just before driving up to see Swindon win the Herefordshire Senior Cup in a 4 - 2 penalty shoot-out following a 2 - 2 draw with Hereford United, I was given the opportunity to dress up again. Peter the Crocodile was now a part of my past now I was a Cyberman! A local company were doing charity work and had a load of Dr Who items including several cybermen from the 25th Anniversary story Silver Nemesis. Knowing my part in the crocodile costume I was approached and asked if I fancy feeling a pratt again and dressing up but for charity. As I have been known to do odd things including throwing myself out of aircraft (with parachute) for charity I
accepted. The suit was a bit of a tight fit and the helmet a bit claustrophobic, but it had a fibre glass back panel for easy escape in case of emergency. The event was a success and I repeated the exercise at a similar charity occasion. I was given the costume on the basis I did a couple more events for them. I did including getting to meet Jon Pertwee, Nicholas Courtney and the rest of the cast from Dr Who when they filmed a special show in nearby Aldbourne on the anniversary of the original show The Daemons being filmed. The location being Aldbourne, Membury airfield and surrounding areas. I was not however, a Cyberman on that day! I fulfilled my obligations and kept the suit. To start with in the spare room, which Christopher took over and having had a few nightmares about it, I moved it to the

dining room. Eventually I sold it at Auction to clear a few debts after receiving a lot of justified grief from Teresa about the kids being scared stiff of the monster. The neighbours all thought I was completely round the twist having the costume in the house on a mannequin dummy. Perhaps they were right?

Next stop was Bournemouth. Charlton were playing their and won 1 - 0 thanks to a well taken goal by John Robinson. I arranged to meet some fans from London whom I met at the Torquay Friendly. They had gone to Devon for a week's holiday then saw the Middlesbrough friendly advertised and appeared wearing their Charlton shirts at the match. After meeting up they went to the terraces whilst I went to the stand. Sitting in the front row I had my view blocked by Kim Grant and Mike Ammann who were Charlton's Subs that day. I passed a couple of comments and the second half was a very friendly one with both of them sat directly in front of me watching the game and talking to me at the same time.

Andy completed his 300th consecutive Oxford game with the home match against Peterborough United in the Coca Cola Cup 1st Round, quite ironic as Peterborough were sponsored by Debbie's company, Thomas Cook. He had missed the earlier testimonial match with Aston Villa which I had attended but as it was not an official league or cup match it did not count! Well that was his excuse anyway. Given the choice I would probably have done the same thing and been on holiday in Kos!

Swindon adventured into the Anglo Italian cup which they had won years ago. The new Intel stand was now open and several season ticket holders around us had defected over to the other side. Mel decided he wanted to try it out so we sat over there for the first half. He hated it as he found it steep and dangerous. He was later to be proved right as during the winter I saw a fan slip and fall along way down the steps in the icy weather. Mel decided that he wanted to go back to the North Stand. He was adamant about it and ran into trouble as Stewards refused to transfer him, being a brother of a director or not! Mike Hughes the Stadium Manager managed to sort the problem out when I called him over and we walked along the pitch to the other side during the half time interval much to the confusion of the onlooking crowd. Town lost the game 2 - 0, but bounced back with a 1 - 0 victory over Watford a few days later!

Devon was calling and Mike wanted to talk business over Christmas supplies so I was more than happy to pop down. I ended up talking shop for quite some time and stayed overnight at his main hotel, but only after taking in The Gulls 2 - 1 win over Northampton.

Below: Dr Who on location in Aldbourne for the anniversary video. And the cause of much merriment amongst the neighbours as a Cyberman.

Matchball Sponsorships then started to occur as part of business packages I had sold into clubs. The first at Oxford United was for the 1 - 1 draw with Birmingham City on 10th September 1994. The club have looked after me ever since and business is always conducted based on sponsorships being built into the price of contracts sold in. To date I have been back to sample arguably one of the best clubs in the leagues sponsorship package 6 times, the latest on 30th November 1996 was probably the most amusing when Charlton played at the Manor Ground. Charlton officials had taken their full allocation of seats in the directors box and several extra sponsors were putting money into the club. My group which included Paul Clayton who writes in the Charlton programme were moved over to the Manor Club and served a buffet. As the hospitality girls, Claire and the lovely Molly were running around like headless chickens trying to look after everyone over two buildings Gary spent some time with us before giving me the drinks vouchers and being left to fend for ourselves. Being an old pro at this by now and well known to most behind the scenes at the club it was not a problem temporarily being attached to the club on the commercial side to look after guests. Andy had missed out on the buffet preferring to go to the Butchers Arms with his mates. He turned up just prior to kick off then said he preferred his own seat and left joining us briefly at half time for a coffee. As he takes his football so seriously it was not a surprise to find him not turn up after the match which Charlton Athletic had won 2 - 0 for the post match buffet of photo session with the players. He had taken the result so much to heart that on arriving in the players lounge shortly afterwards I found all his friends still drinking but he had left shortly after the final whistle with his friend Lisa. When I spoke to him the following Monday he said he was so fed up he went straight home! Well at least I enjoyed the day and the result.

Several more games at the County Ground and the Manor passed without incident before Charlton visited Swindon in the Coca Cola cup. It was best remembered for Charlton winning 3 - 1 and my jumping in the air with delight at the 3rd goal much to the disgust of my fellow season ticket holders sat around me. Town were still riding high in the First Division, but they were soon to enter freefall and just managed to be relegated on the final week of the league season. This was probably the last time I had a long chat with my colleague Gary Nelson. Ever since it has been brief conversations in passing, as his business Gary Nelson Enterprises was starting to take off! His picture framing side had a contract to supply items at the club shop at Charlton, he had started to take journalism more seriously and had started to write a book which has since become a best seller called Left Foot Forward. His friend Chris Carter was at the match and Gary was staying with him overnight to visit old friends in the town and go night clubbing afterwards. Chris's daughter Sascha was to become a Swindon cheerleader the following season as a "Robinette".

To-ing and fro-ing between the Manor and County ground took up most of my time for the next two months. Jan Aage Fjortoft had at last found his scoring touch and produced some memorable goals. Against Brighton in the Coca Cola Cup 3rd Round Replay Fraser Digby kicked the ball from his goal area which crossed the half way line bounced and Jan hit it on the volley into the Brighton net. He followed this up with another spectacular effort against Millwall in the next round of the cup as well.

The end of November saw me spend a fortnight in Manchester on business, I was in the middle of doing surveys for Stoll Moss Theatres and Apollo Leisure on First Aid and Safety requirements. A trip to London the previous week had me on stage at all the top theatres, watching rehearsals for Starlight Express and Phantom of the Opera whilst walking amongst the actors putting them off their lines. On one stage I was checking the state and position of a first aid box in the crew room and got in the way of two people on stage rehearsing, One of them turned round and asked what I was up to wandering around with the theatre manager. I didn't recognise him but was later told he was Tony Slattery. That day was full of incidents like that. Having just come off stage at the Dominion Theatre having sat by the car used as a prop in Grease, doing paperwork, I was considering the quickest route to Victoria Station to the Apollo Victoria Theatre when Boyzone, the pop group ran into me literally. They were across the road in Virgin Records doing a signing session, had just finished and were trying to escape their teenage fans when I was knocked flying. One of the boys in a clear Irish accent apologised and gave me a couple of their CDs which were in his hands. He was very genuine and a complete opposite from the brush I had with Take That. One of my neighbours daughters loves the group so I gave her one of the CDs which made her day.

Manchester beckoned and in between driving around the city getting lost, which I tend to do with regularity even when going in via the Knutsford Services exit on the M6 or via the M62 which takes you into Salford. I completed my work in the area and managed to take a look at some players for Dennis Smith. My first stop was at Manchester United for their Youth Cup 2nd Round game with Wrexham which they won 4 - 1. I was amazed that even for this type of game the club draws in crowds in the thousands. Stockport County then took on and beat Scarborough 3 - 1 in the Autowindscreens Shield 2nd Round. It was cold that night and I had worked late to complete an area of calls so didn't have time to go back to the hotel and change. Dressed only in a suit I froze and in the end purchased a Stockport County sweatshirt from the club shop in a bid to keep myself warm. I actually like the quality of that shirt and on occasions wear it out in public gaining several odd looks from passers by. The strangest look and comment I have received was one Sunday when I took the kids swimming at the Oasis Leisure Centre in Swindon. We were queuing to get in and I was wearing one of my Alloa shirts. A comment was raised by someone else in the queue who asked who Alloa were, on telling him I received the reply no one supports teams like that in England. No sooner had he finished the sentence when a gentleman walked up the stairs from the changing rooms wearing a blue Montrose FC shirt. His timing was perfect!

Using my football contacts I managed to get a ticket for the Manchester City v Newcastle United Coca Cola 4th Round tie which was a sell out. I knew Oxford would be unable to afford anything that was on show so spent the evening enjoying the 1 - 1 draw and wandering if my car was still in one piece being left parked in Moss Side. Fortunately the company car was unscratched and unharmed!

I moved across to Bolton to see the Wanderers beat Port Vale 1 - 0. I remember the evening very well, as having been invited into the pub opposite the ground which was deemed Home supporters only I enjoyed the Northern hospitality to its fullest, however, on leaving the pub to cross the road I felt hungry and was ripped off by the extorsionate price of £2 for a cheeseburger. This vendor must have learnt his trade at Wembley or Old Trafford! Having made the purchase to quieten my noisy stomach I found my seat in the stand and again froze. The old wooden stand with its antiquated hut inside which doubled up as a tea stall was most appealing. Having queued for about 15 minutes I was eventually served with a hot Bovril. On leaving the queue a large gentleman exited the toilets opposite and knocked the drink flying some of it over me. This was not the warming sensation I wanted to feel and had to rejoin the queue again for a further 10 minutes to get my drink missing part of the second half.

Returning home is always something of a mystery to me as I never know what I will find. Caryn always looks after the house and visits every day to feed the fish and clear the post from the doorway and to sort out the pet from hell! I have a psychotic cat which although both Christopher and Deborah love it, it drives me up the wall! Its habits are comparable to Men Behaving Badly on TV. The Kids call it Henry although I tend to call it several other names! Whenever I have friends round he cuddles up to them before emitting obnoxious vapours when the guest is least expecting it. If I then throw him out into the conservatory he knocks on the patio door and howls. This is most annoying at about 5 am when he decides he wants to come in having finished his daily ritual of tearing the sofa to shreds in the conservatory. If he has no response he knows my bedroom window is two foot above the conservatory roof so up he jumps and serenades me until I give in. I have two ponds one has been emptied of fish by this creature. I restocked with trout from the local fish farm and put nets over to protect the fish. No good three went missing and I found half a trout behind the sofa. I caught the animal pulling up a steak with his teeth then crawling under the net to get to his pray. Bricks weighted the nets sufficiently to deter him so he has changed his attentions to frogs. I often hear the squeals and go to find him in the conservatory playing with a frog he had captured and brought home to play with. He has also caused me personal injury on more than one occasion by sneaking into the bathroom when I am washing my hair, jumping up at the side of the bath missing the edge and landing claws open onto my groin. The soggy muggy is living on borrowed time! He also takes revenge out on items of furniture if he is displeased. I was doing a cassette for the car, sat infront of the CD player taping when in he strolled curled up next to me and dropped one, with my eyes watering I told him to go away he then decided to try to drink from my can of lager and sneezed into it. After removing him he returned and sneaked behind the TV and ate part of my Stereo speaker and Superwoofer wires so they don't work very well now. This creature has caused me more stress than my ex wife and that is saying something! I am getting a complex over a darn cat. If anyone remembers Jasper Carrot's Mole sketch, well its getting to that extreme although the thought of sitting in the garden on a revolving stool in the middle of the night with a flashlight attached to a 12 bore to protect my fish has crossed my mind, I doubt if I would go to that extreme, just borrow my next door neighbours catapult instead perhaps?

I got home to find the creature had sneaked in whilst Caryn had been feeding it and as a result been locked in the house for about 24 hours. I smelt were he had been, but fortunately the rest of my furniture had remained intact.

Christmas came and went. This year was worse than my first year on my own as Teresa had decided to withdraw access out of spite so I could not take them to the usual Boxing Day family gathering. Access was reinstated when I got back so she could get at the presents given to the kids by my family. She went to great lengths to cause me as much pain as possible. I am pleased to say that although she still has her moments when I could string her up she has grown up and behaves more like an adult and calmed down a lot.

Marlow came to the County Ground for the 3rd Round of the FA Cup, Andy and his mates descended on the club and sat on the Stratton Bank with a lot of other Oxford fans by a large banner saying "Oxford United FC Supporters on loan to Marlow".

Marlow had beaten Oxford in the earlier round so as they had no fixture decided to carry on their hate campaign against Swindon. Swindon won the game 2 - 0 and Lisa, Roger, Les and Richard went home via the nearest half a dozen pubs with Andy to drown their sorrows.

Three days later Swansea visited the Manor for the Autoshield Quarter Final as it was so cold Andy decided we would forsake the Beech Road Stand and all huddle together in the London Road Terrace, it was also convenient for exiting to the players lounge for half time. Funnily enough it was warmer than being in the stand, but the weather was so extreme even Lisa and Andy decided that with Swansea winning 2 - 1 with 10 minutes to go they couldn't face extra time and wished the game away. Oxford did not score an equaliser and the few thousand who bothered to turn up went away very quickly to warm up after the final whistle.

Work site surveys then took me to Devon and Apollo's two theatres in Torquay and Paignton. This was now becoming home from home as I managed to build up a good little area of business down in the Torbay region and stayed with Mike and Barbara Morgan, who were about to extend their hotel chain to three hotels with the purchase of the Kistor Hotel in Belgrave Road, just off the sea front. Both the theatres had a beautiful Assistant Manageress to cover the two sites called Wendy Hughes, Paul Cook, the buyer at Apollo knew I fancied Wendy and made a thing of my visits for a while, she later came to Swindon to manage the Wyvern Theatre before returning to Manage the Torbay sites. I missed my chance with her - story of my life really! The trip was now a set routine which included United's ground and Ted Owens who ran the Catering Franchise at Plainmoor as well as other coffee houses in Newton Abbott and Alan Grinsill who managed the bars in the Boots and Laces restaurant. This bar and restaurant is probably the best in the lower divisions for service, layout and presentation and worth a visit when in the area even if not for a game. (Plug over to keep Cedric Munslow, the Commercial Manager happy!). The trip was then always finished off with a detour to Stoke Canon, a village just outside Exeter to see Debbie's dad Les and drop off and collect things for Debs.

Swindon reached the Coca Cola Cup Semi finals and beat Bolton 2 - 1 at home before losing on aggregate following an exciting Bolton comeback late into the second leg at Burnden Park.

Andy's daughter Rachel had never been to a match and Debbie was a Crystal Palace supporter in the past so when Bristol Rovers played Oxford on 18th February we all went together for Rachel's first match. A boring 0 - 0 draw was the result, enough to put any young supporter off going to a game!

This game was followed by an even worse performance as Swindon and Barnsley went to sleep using Oldham tactics and another 0 - 0 ensued. The goal drought was to come to an abrupt end with Stockport County playing at Oxford, having a warped sense of humour I wore the Stockport sweatshirt and received a few mutterings from Lisa who was now starting to accept my presence. Whilst being known as a Swindon season ticket holder I am tolerated as I have said earlier but that night I saw the look of shear panic on Andy's face! It was cold and I only had two scarves one Charlton, the other Swindon. So I brought along the Swindon one to keep me warm, Andy saw it whilst having a pint in the Butchers Arms and asked

"Why do I have a death wish wearing that around the Manor?"

As Swindon were not playing against United I foresaw no reason to worry, however, I removed it and put it round Andy's neck. He quickly panicked and removed it from sight before the locals saw it.

Feelings of hate run deep in Oxford, pity really as although rivalry is good for competition, going to the extremes that some supporters do by showing hatred is only bad for the game. I have only ever noticed resentment to that extent once before, when standing in the Shed at Chelsea whilst they played Millwall!

Renewing old acquaintances with Roy King and Steve Dixon at Charlton's 2 - 1 defeat at Bristol City proceeded a return trip to Scotland on business and to see a young player in the Scottish League for Dennis, he turned out not to be as recommended and played a dreadful match as St Mirren drew 0 - 0 with St Johnstone in the 1st Division. I managed to get to Recreation Park and meet up with George Ormiston and Willie McKie who introduced me to Peter Gibson who was now looking after the commercial side of the club. Douglas Lawrie my old schoolfriend, now a player, arrived at the ground at the same time I did and it was as if the clock had been turned back a few years with instant recognition and a long chat. The old wooden Stand had been demolished after burning down and been replaced by a modern stand which although very much based on the old layout but with increased offices and dining areas in the back, the seating capacity is on the small side. The Taylor Report had hit the club badly, Once having a capacity of over 13, 000, but reduced to 10, 000 when I was with Alloa. The new maximum had been reduced to just over 4, 000 with areas by the covered terrace opposite the stand fenced off for safety reasons. Given the crowds that go rarely will this trouble the club, but it means that big games have to be staged away or in cases of playing Celtic in the League Cup at the start of 1996 - 97 season transferring to Partick Thistle so 12, 000 can watch the game in safety.

After being shown around the small but impressive stand I joined the team in the dressing room prior to the Reserve match with East Fife. Most of the team were youngsters but a recognised former player appeared on the bench as "trialist" and scored from the penalty spot in the last kick of the game when Alloa won 4 - 1!

Although it was by now March, I was still having trouble getting re acclimatised to the United Kingdom's weather having spent an enjoyable holiday in the Philippines with temperatures in the 90's at its coldest point! I had travelled over to attend a Philippine wedding with a friend before having a holiday on the White sands of Boracay Island, Asia's top beach resort. No one had prepared me for what I was to find in that country! Most of the women are beautiful and unmaterialistic, they exist to look after the male species such is their way of life, I was in my element! Having arrived on time at the airport and finding my hotel in Manila I went for a stroll round the block which was next to the American Embassy, This used to be a former red light district until the Americans moved their Air Force base to Angeles to the north of the capital. On arriving back at the hotel, the doorman was carrying a firearm. He told me it was the norm in Manila and cash exchange centres had security guards dressed like Rambo with pump action shotguns a minimum requirement. Whilst most Philippine people are the most friendly of people in the world it is also a poor place with more than its fair share of problems. I had had a lucky escape walking were I had with my travellers cheques on me as a western tourist had been murdered for their money round the corner several days previously. I was on my guard for the rest of the trip. Women threw them selves at me before during and after the wedding I was in a position of having my friend and her cousin openly fighting over me! Rose was a lovely shy girl and her cousin just as beautiful. The only problem was her parents who kept asking how much money I had Etc. To marry a westerner is the ultimate in their lives and moves the family to important status amongst their groups, unfortunately whilst Rose was very genuine and loved me all I could see was a materialistic family behind her and was not about to be used again and backed off. Leila, but better known as Lye was different as she had a better paid job than myself and was better educated, her family were worried about me incase their daughter was hurt, but were kind and caring and did not think too much about status, they wanted me to move to Manila rather than take their daughter away from them or them move to England. It was perfect and after a wonderful holiday decided I would love to live in Boracay or Dakak and own my own hotel and promote it back in this country. The only problem was I was unable to accept the possibility of not seeing Deborah and Christopher, so turned my back on paradise to be near my children.

The beach was ideal with a hotel bedroom which led onto the sands, Lye was over tired one night so whilst she went back to bed I wandered up to visit the local bars and saw the customary Germans on the beach drinking at one of the bars. I was wearing my Charlton Athletic team shirt and it was recognised by one of the tourists so after a quick bottle of beer the 1966 World Cup Final was restaged on White Beech on the other side of the world by a few football fanatics using a coconut as a ball much to the confusion of the natives. I returned several hours later covered in sand and received a telling off from Lye who was convinced some of the other native girls had taken me away from her. We got engaged whilst out their, but getting a visa was impossible. So ended that relationship!

The Philippines have just started to take up football after having Baseball and Boxing dominate for years with the American influence over there. My spot of playing on the beech was probably a first for the country as I sat with the Philippine FA Delegate on the plane home. He was going to Lancaster Gate for a meeting about furthering the sport, however, from the conversation I had with him it transpired that he was chosen as the best man for the job having seen the game played in other countries. I have visions of Zaire's football team in the 1974 World Cup Finals who didn't know the rules of the game reappearing through the Philippines now playing in their first World Cup qualifying games!

Gary returned to Swindon for Charlton's 1 - 0 victory over Town, The locals had by now got used to the idea that they had a non supporter in their ranks especially Patrick whom I normally sit next to along with Mel and Kevin. Town's slide down the table was gathering momentum, so the defeat was dismissed as par for the course as supporters were starting to get accustomed to the thought of the possibility of 2nd Division football. It was later said to me by another club:

"It must be exciting watching Swindon, as you never know what Division the team will be playing in from one season to the next!"
Quite true in hindsight as Town have not played in the same division two season's running since their promotion to the Premiership.

As Debbie's birthday and mine are only two days apart, I celebrated my 30th Birthday on Deb.'s 31st on the 4th April by going out for a meal with both her and Caryn turning down Andy's invitation to join him at the Manor were Wrexham were playing. He did not want to join in the meal as it would end his run of consecutive matches, such is the dominance the sport has over his life!

We had a drink on Easter Monday in High Wycombe before United lost 1 - 0, though as I was driving I did not indulge myself too much. Taxi's to the ground but walking back was exhausting, I learnt my lesson about parking in the Industrial Estate the previous year were I was stuck in the traffic bottleneck for 3/4 hour. Paul Lowe, one of the Directors who drinks with Andy's mates had a ticket for the club car park and was surprised we did not join him by parking in the ground. He later found out why!

The last visit to Devon of the season proved to be a damp squib with a 0 - 0 draw against Exeter City, but a point won against the nearest and dearest is better than a point lost! Then up to Bromsgrove to meet Elaine Jowett and the Halifax Town team as previously mentioned. Four more Swindon matches of mixed results finished with the visit of Charlton Reserves. An Apollo Leisure employee I recognised arrived to support Athletic proudly boasting that although Sheffield Wednesday had Tango Man, he was Charlton's equivalent being known as Pie Man. It takes all sorts! He was a different person when I visited the night-club where he worked in Oxford, probably after realising what a twit he had appeared as.

Earlier in the season, Andrew Cove one of the buyers for Morlands Brewery in Abingdon had let slip that he was a Reading supporter and had stood in the same spot on the covered terrace under the clock at Elm Park since his first match many years ago, as had his dad and his dad before him, so when Reading played at the County Ground I entertained both him and his two sons in the executive lounge. He was late owing to traffic and missed the meal so I ate with Glenn Hoddle and John Gorman's wife Myra instead. When Andrew finally arrived his sons went in search of autographs whilst I had the sensation of feeling someone else's hands in my pockets whilst talking to Andrew. Andrea Elliott who works at the club and knows me very well was selling draw tickets and was fondling for loose change. It was one way of drumming up business but I never asked if she had found what she was looking for, but she later turned me down when I asked her out on a date!

To reciprocate Morland Brewery own the Spread Eagle pub opposite the Reading ground and I was invited over for a drink prior to the Charlton home match on 7th May. I sat in the stand amongst a Liverpool and Sheffield Wednesday Scout and just behind Steve Dixon. The scouts were looking at Lee Bowyer who was to later sign for Leeds United. Charlton lost 2 - 1 to close the league season.

I finished off the season with a return to Wembley for the 5 a side tournament to see Wycombe Wanderers successfully reclaim the trophy following a 1 - 0 penalty shoot-out after a 0 - 0 draw. The events of the previous years tournament were not to be repeated as the organisers had learnt their lessons and segregated Sam Hamman and any other would be antagonists to other areas where no one could be offended by anyone else's actions.

Chapter 15
Seasoned Traveller

The 1995 - 96 season kicked off in glorious sunshine at Finchampstead Road Wokingham were Town drew 0 - 0 with a Sheffield United side which included few first teamers. Roy Merryweather continued to give my company support and we continued our arrangement and for the continued orders I took out match and player sponsorship packages. Knowing me as well guaranteed cash on delivery for deliveries whilst others had to wait as the club was getting deeper into debt due to the lack of support being given to the club, both by the supporters and the council who were constantly turning down planning applications within the town boundaries for the ground to be relocated. Selling the ground was the way forward for the club who could not expand much further as they had the Reading to Waterloo railway line at one end of the ground and the Reading to Tunbridge Wells/ Gatwick line at the other. The remaining two sides being sealed off by the two lines merging approaching the station and the main Finchampstead Road. Being a reasonable size it was perfect for a supermarket and a buyer was interested, but the locals were unhappy about having a club on their doorstep and placed opposition to each application submitted. It is a catch 22 situation, the club could be lost as a result and people forget that it is a major part of the community. Roy has teams entered in all the junior leagues from Under 10's upwards and a lot of parents watch their children playing. Take the club away and 100's of children will be without something they enjoy to keep themselves occupied so possibly leading to troublesome bored hooligans in the future. The locals at all clubs throughout the country need to support their local team not Manchester United because they always win. If you were to ask the average 6 year old
"Where do Manchester United play?"
the common reply will probably be:

"On TV!"

Where as Sky put a lot into the game in terms of revenue it is taken by the fat cats of the league and little feeds through to the lower divisions, added to the issue over my former team mate John Bosman where lower clubs used to rely on transfer fees to keep them selves afloat this is now put into serious jeopardy with the Bosman Ruling and clubs will probably start folding in large numbers by the year 2000. I have often been asked why I dedicate my life to the lower leagues and not watch the Premier Division. My answer is clear. If people don't follow my lead and clubs fold where will the new players of quality come from. Lee Sharpe was signed from Torquay United by Manchester United. Had it not been for the Gulls being in existence then Lee may never have had his chance to shine at the top level. Without the smaller clubs providing quality players their is a danger of the league becoming full of imports and no quality English players emerging. Without them We will never win the World Cup again! Think about it. Ice Hockey has expanded in this country and taken full use of the Bosman ruling. The English youngsters are not getting a chance to play because of the talent coming in from overseas. This sport could be the first to collapse and foreign mercenaries would be all that would be on show as the kids will have lost interest as they were not given support and failed to get into the teams. The mercenaries cost more than youngsters so bringing the club down. In recent years Ice Hockey has lost Milton Keynes Kings and nearly Peterborough Pirates this year, others have given up professional Leagues preferring to stage junior games as finances can not support a decent team in the senior league.

The Wokingham Physio David Lane has numerous contacts including Brentford and was keen to put together a first aid package to offer the clubs on block as direct competition to Medisport who were supplying bespoke items to the clubs and charging over the top for it as no one else was prepared to look down this avenue because clubs were notoriously bad payers and judged a business risk. I had put together a large package worth over £2, 500 to Oxford United for first aid supply to the catering sites. The team were under a separate contract, so financially it made sense to press on. I took this idea further and several other clubs accepted the arrangement, however, it was at this point in mid season when the company I was contracted to had a major reshuffle and I found myself out of a job. The personal side of my company expanded to include discount airline flight tickets as well as a Sales and Marketing Consultancy. But I could only really expand with help or an input of cash. Having been taken for a ride by a few other companies recently and losing a lot of money I found myself in a catch 22 position with little to invest and not prepared to get any loans to worsen the heavy millstone round my neck. But if the money was present I could make a success of it. I approached a few other companies about coming in with me on the first aid idea and found the hesitancy because of the risk factor involved with the clubs. So whilst putting it to one side and hoping to do something positive in the future about it I kept the company ticking over whilst looking for another job back in paid employment. I found that I was over qualified for most jobs and even office positions as a manager could lead to problems with all the politics and backstabbing that goes on, as managers were afraid to take me on knowing I have been so successful in the past I could be a threat to their own careers but their directors dismissing them in favour of myself. I got extremely frustrated and when Don O'Riordan was sacked as manager at Plainmoor applied for the vacant position. Mike Bateson, the chairman offered this to Eddie May and after consulting John James the chief Scout I was brought in to assist Eddie with the scouting for Torquay United reporting directly to John, who in turn compiled reports for Eddie.

I went to MDS Training in Swindon and was given a short term contract to assist with the teaching and training of adults in the basics of Information Technology. After assisting to write and prepare a City and Guilds level one course it was put into practice and I had 6 happy months with them training. I gained an NVQ Level 2 in Using Information Technology thanks to the support of my colleague Peter

Burke. It would have been a level 3 but for the fact that the company were not authorised at that point to teach to that standard by the City and Guilds. It was a pity I could not extend the contract, but at least I came out from it with a further qualification and even more experience to make me even more over qualified!

Wokingham Town had signed a striker called Steve Darlington from Staines Town, he was the leagues top goalscorer and reminded me a lot of Rodney Jack at Torquay. He in fact finished the season as the league's top goalscorer again with 41 goals from 52 appearances in 95 - 96 season. I told Eddie about him, but he was sceptical about buying at Isthmian /ICIS League level. Having signed Jamie Nadh from fellow side Kingstonian didn't seem to make much difference, so a quality player fell through my fingers! At the end of the season Wokingham couldn't hang onto him and Kingstonian snapped him up like a shot. When Kevin Hodges took over at Torquay I again brought up the subject of Steve, but by that time both Kevin and Gary had brought in a few new faces and Mike Bateson had put a stop on player purchases.

July saw Deborah attending her first match. Cirencester Town at home to a Swindon Town X1 in a friendly. Despite the 0 - 0 scoreline both kids loved going for different reasons. Christopher for retrieving the Matchball for Steve Mildenhall, the Swindon Youth goalkeeper who made his day by talking to him, and Deborah for the warm evening and being able to run on the pitch at half time to release some of her energy. It was difficult trying to explain that she couldn't do that at the County Ground later on in the season.

After the theatres came Apollo Leisure's Cinema and Bingo Hall division, so I was off on my travels again. The McCain Stadium in Scarborough being a good point for a stopover as they played York City in an Eastern Electricity Cup Final losing 1 - 0 to a hotly disputed penalty awarded by an inexperienced referee handling his second ever match since being promoted to the league's list of official referees. I had a disagreement with the "Comedian" Roy Chubby Brown whilst in the town for using his official car parking space whilst in the theatre, as the spot was in a back alley behind the theatre it caused a lot of problems reversing out just to keep him happy. As it was just into August the tourists were out in force, but being by the seaside was relaxing so across country I travelled to Blackpool. I was wary of this town as car clampers lie in wait for unsuspecting tourists. I had become a victim of them on a previous visit, but escaped on this occasion. A 2 - 2 draw with Wigan in the Lancashire Marsden Cup Final brought the Latics foreign duo of Martinez and Diaz to my attention and I would love to get them down to Plainmoor to play for the Gulls but sadly we can't afford them. The journey home was broken in Bradford with a friendly against Manchester United which proved to be very profitable for the Bantams as a sell out occurred and the capacity crowd saw United win 1 - 0.

So to the start of the league season and up to Birmingham to see West Brom beat Charlton in a very unsatisfactory manner. The Birmingham Road Terrace had been demolished in the summer and a new stand built in its place. I was given a piece of terrace nicely varnished and mounted with a plaque on a wooden plinth. A limited edition which number was 111. I was highly impressed at the commercialism at the Albion and how they turned worthless rubble into a profit making venture. Perhaps a few other clubs should follow their example when building work is carried out.

The following week it was a return to Lancashire and an attempted football comeback. I saw Rochdale defeat York 2 - 1 in the Coca Cola Cup and a chance meeting led me to train with the Rochdale team at their Spotland ground and try out for them. This was an eye opener as Day one was the nearest I have experienced to attempting to kill myself! I was out of condition in a big way but surprisingly still had retained some ball control. I literally crawled off the pitch at the end of the day.

The Manager was sacked the same day and for Day two the coach tookover and to say everything was in a state of confusion would be an understatement. The day ended with the directors looking at the team and deciding what to do in the interim period, before a replacement was found for the manager's position. I left as it was deemed I would not have been good enough to play for the team. Was I a victim of circumstances? Possibly, but realistically my time had passed as a serious footballer and I was best left to concentrate on efforts behind the scenes. I left Spotland with a smile grateful for at least having had another chance and a signed football from my colleagues as a personal momento of the occasion. On leaving I headed for Chester and their Pontins League Division Three match against Bury Reserves. Although Bury won 4 - 2 I didn't see anything too spectacular from an individual, but for novelty sake moved around the ground at half time so I can say I saw the first half of the match in England and the second half in Wales.

On getting home Swindon Town were in action against York City in a 2nd Division match and I was starting to get very used to their players especially Paul Baker who had been scoring very regularly in the first team, although he was unable to do so on this occasion with the Robins winning 3 - 0.

Two more Coca Cola matches followed at Swindon and Oxford before going to Scotland for 3 days on business. I managed to see a match on each evening, all three being in the Scottish Coca Cola Cup 3rd Round. Airdrie beating Hibs 2 - 0 was a non event, but visiting Ibrox to see the changes made since my previous visit was exciting and I became very impressed with the layout of the club and its facilities. Watching them defeat Alloa's arch rivals Stirling 3 - 2 added some spice to the evening, but the highlight was my last night in Glasgow. Celtic's return to Parkhead following a season at Hampden whilst their ground was being rebuilt. The new tall imposing stand increased the capacity but obtaining a ticket for the game was impossible. That is unless you have contacts. Fortunately I did and felt privileged to be part of the emotional occasion. The game finished in a 1 - 1 draw but Celtic scored in extra time to go through. August had now past and already I had attended 16 senior games. This was to be a mammoth season when I was to surpass my previous records and attend 116 senior matches.

September started with a return to the Manor Ground for a Matchball sponsorship with that club again York City! I had now seen them 4 times in the space of 4 weeks, but at least I got to see Paul Baker in action again. The game was televised live on Central TV and was Robin Herd's first match as the new Chairman of Oxford United. He was late arriving so delaying a TV interview, but when he arrived we were treated to one of the all time classics on quotes from TV presenter Tony Frances, who said:

"I suppose it was bound to happen that the new chairman missed the plane, especially when the last one missed the boat!"

The comment was met with great mirth from the boardroom and Andy got to discuss it with Robin whilst they were both in the Gents together. Oxford won the game 2 - 0.

Another couple of days in Scotland followed as I worked hard to achieve some hard targets set for me, but managed to renew my acquaintances with Alex Totten, but only in passing as Kilmarnock were giving a big press release and Alex didn't have much time available. I stayed on to watch their reserve side draw 0 - 0 with Motherwell. Rugby Park has changed beyond recognition from my last visit with Alloa back in 1979. The all seater stadium is as impressive as Ibrox and a credit to the club. I was staying in Busby a small village just outside Castlemilk on the border of Glasgow which made Hampden Park only ten minutes drive away, so after finishing work I was able to nip back to the hotel and get changed before going to the Stadium to see Scotland beat Finland 1 - 0 in the European Championship Qualifying Group 8 match. I sat with London's Burning Actor John Alford for a while before he had to move on when it emerged he was sitting in the wrong seat. Opening my mouth proved a problem as John's replacement asked to see my programme as he couldn't get one. On handing it over and telling him there was no score I heard a grunt behind me:

"A bloody Sasanach!"

was the comment and I then had to endure the Neanderthal man joking to his mates about the English and feeling his boots digging in my back through the gap in the back rest of the seat. This did not stop when Scotland scored the only goal and I cheered with everyone else as I was supporting a British country, still I half expected to find I would receive treatment like that from someone whilst spending so much time back in the country. I did find a terrific Indian restaurant in a small row of shops opposite the ground and it made a change from Hotel cuisine although I was growing fond of the Busby Hotel's speciality of Sirloin Steak served with stilton cheese melted on top with fried onions flombayed in brandy at the table. I tried cooking the meal at home but it did not quite taste the same!

Back home and two more Swindon league games passed along with Oxford's Coca Cola cup draw at home to QPR. Then followed Swindon's Coca Cola game with Blackburn Rovers. Town scored twice in two minutes to totally dominate most of the game before Alan Shearer woke up and produced a dazzling display which destroyed Town and Rovers eventually won 3 - 2.

The following day my company was holding a meeting in the midlands which included overnight accommodation, so I took full advantage to sneak away to see another Pontins League Division 3 match, this time being a 1 - 1 draw between Coventry City Reserves and Port Vale reserves, but no one special stood out and it broke the monotony of Swindon games. Town were however, leading the 2nd Division and increased their lead with a 1 - 0 win over Rotherham United. I chose to watch as I was fed up of driving and had another trip to Scotland lined up for the whole of the following week. Five games in five days was taking the scouting job seriously whilst completing all my other work tasks on time. I slept through most of the Saturday when I got home that weekend. After watching Dundee lose at home to Stenhousemuir in the Challenge Cup Quarter Final, It was off to see another Quarter Final but this time at Clydebank who lost to Dundee's next door neighbours Dundee United 1 - 0. Now getting into the swing of things I checked on a defender playing for Clyde in a reserve match at the Broadwood Stadium in Cumbernauld. Clyde's manager Alex Smith recognised me and we watched the game from the executive box. Just as well really as a cold northern wind was blowing round the stadium and it was bitterly cold. Not only that, this Reserve Cup Match finished in a draw and a further 30 minutes were played. The sides were still together at 1 - 1 so it went to penalty kicks which Clyde won 5 - 4. I was very impressed with the defender who had started out as a centre forward before Alex moved him back to defence and I have him up my sleeve on a shortlist in case Kevin Hodges ever wants a defender/ utility man. Alex asked me to stay behind for a drink and chat, but unfortunately because of the extra time and penalties my time was short as I had to return to Ibrox as I was given a ticket for Rangers UEFA Champions League match with Borrussia Dortmond and I had no intention of missing that match, as it was for pleasure only. The idea of Paul Gascoigne signing for Oxford or Torquay is great, but the wages would bankrupt both clubs very quickly!

Celtic were playing their midweek matches on a Thursday and I was grateful for that fact as having enjoyed the 2 - 2 draw at Ibrox, my contact who got me the Parkhead ticket a month earlier came up trumps again and took me to see the 4 - 0 European Cup Winners Cup win over Dinamo Batumi.

I was totally exhausted by the time I arrived home late on Friday evening and did not bother with a match on the Saturday, preferring to catch up on some lost sleep as my Sundays were busy looking after the kids. 3am Monday morning it was back up north and I was on auto pilot driving up the M74 towards Glasgow, but this was to be my last week in Scotland before the company reshuffle and loss of contract. So I had to return to Alloa that night and sit with Peter Gibson in the stand whilst watching the reserves playing and beating Berwick Rangers 4 - 0. They were managed by my old friend Ian Smith and we had quite a long chat after the match. He was a little embarrassed when I told him I had found the photo produced elsewhere in this book, but he was always a bit of a character!

Partick Thistle's 1 - 1 draw in the Premier League with Kilmarnock was the final match and getting home now contractless brought mixed emotions. The loss of the company car was to hurt most as it kept my scouting expenses to a minimum. But after Swindon's 2 - 0 win over Bristol City I purchased a car as a cheap run around but have since changed several times until I arrived at my current car which is my pride and joy. A Porsche 924 Turbo which is a very rare beast. Having made only 18, 000 of the vehicle Porsche estimate that less than 3, 000 are still in existence so I will hang onto it.

A boring 0-0 draw at Peterborough for Northampton brought me back to Plainmoor for the first time this season and the Autoglass game against Swindon Town. Martin Ling scored for Swindon in the 1 - 1 draw after going behind. John James agreed that Martin would make a useful addition to the squad and although available was still on Swindon's Premiership wages along with Paul Bodin on £90, 000 per year. They were both released by Town to cut costs at the end of the season. We tried to get Martin, but he had also received offers from a top Malaysian side who were their countries equivalent to Manchester United, but in the end his wife being a Londoner wanted to return to the capital so he signed on for Leyton Orient.

My second sponsorship of the season at Oxford then appeared with a dismal 4 - 1 defeat by Wycombe Wanderers. I was sat next to Sam Hamman in the Directors Box. Remembering Wembley I did try to make conversation with him at one brief point, but unfortunately his attitude remained un changed and he looked passed me as if I didn't exist. I really can't stand rudeness and this guy stands out as one of the rudest I've ever met and that is saying something! The team were so bad that Dennis Smith demanded that they make a public apology for the way they played, And they did!

The Wycombe game also marked a turn in my health for the worst. I was in a lot of pain, by the time I got home and put it down to over indulgence of the free alcohol as I was not driving. It later turned out to be a stomach Ulcer. I should have recognised the symptoms after suffering one with high blood pressure amongst other things when Teresa left me. The alcohol had caused a reaction and inflamed the ulcer causing the pain. I was told by my doctor to cut down which I duly did and the pain and the Ulcer eventually went. This was not to be the last one and in reality suffering another ulcer in 1996 probably saved my life! I recognised the pain and as I was under a lot of stress at the time acted on doctors orders and took my medicine for several weeks, then one Sunday whilst visiting my parents house with the kids I nearly collapsed and had to take to a bed for several hours whilst my mum and dad entertained the kids. They were very worried and what followed was a complete cover up to stop them worrying. I told them I had a severe ulcer which was causing the pain. This part was true, but I kept the rest a secret as they worry a lot about my welfare enough as it is! Whilst I was showing all the symptoms of the Ulcer, I was also showing others which disturbed my doctor including the passing of mucus in my faeces. I was sent to Princess Margaret's Hospital in Swindon for a Barium Meal which found the ulcer and something of a shock! I had a small cancerous growth in the Bowel. If it had not been for the ulcer it would have grown and possibly killed me. As it was in its infancy I was very lucky! What followed was a drawn out process which included radiotherapy, blood tests, numerous visits to the doctor and things shoved into embarrassing places. An enema I can face, but to have a doctor with a warped sense of humour asking me to smile as I bent over was a little too much. It turned out that he was trying to relax me before inserting a hollow metal tube with a small camera in it to look inside to see if the treatment had worked. Air was passed up the tube to make the intestine expand to aid the vision of the camera. It was not the sort of blow job I would recommend, the treatment left me sore!

I confided in Andy and we agreed not to tell Debbie as she would worry, especially as her mother had died from bowel cancer. I thought it strange as I was certain Deb's had told me she died from breast cancer, but as it is still a very sensitive point with her decided not to pursue the issue. I kept the illness from both Debbie and Caryn until I was on the mend, but I think they realised as it is unusual for me to go to the hospital once a year let alone five or six times in a short period. Now it is all behind me if you forgive the pun!

Three scoreless draws followed in Wolverhampton (v Charlton); Bournemouth (v Swindon), and then Blackburn's UEFA Champions League match with Legia Warsaw. The Halloween night's game at Bournemouth led to my Swindon coach jinx striking again. I had arranged to go on the supporters coach and was to be collected from the doctors surgery at the West Swindon District Centre. Only problem was I arrived early and waited at the wrong surgery, as a second surgery by the Link Centre had opened. By the time I realised what had happened I phoned the coach company who phone the coach and found it was past Marlborough and refused to turn round to collect me. A fruitless argument ensued before I ran home to an astonished neighbour who was holding a street barbecue on the driveway and jumped in the car and drove down to the coast. I made it with 10 minutes to spare. Considering the poor game, I would have been better spending my time at the barbecue. A fog then descended on the area and not only was I stuck for over an hour in the one entrance/exit car park waiting to get out, the poor visibility restricted visibility to 10 feet and I drove home very slowly arriving in Swindon in the early hours of the morning mentally and physically exhausted.

Then back to the scouting. I was chasing Colchester United's Mark Kinsella and watched him over several matches. Eddie May then approached United to sign him, but with an asking fee of £300,000 it proved to be too high.

"That's the equivalent of a season's gate receipts!"

was Mike Bateson's response so the approach was dropped. He ended up at Charlton Athletic at the beginning of this season, so perhaps all was not lost as he did sign for one of my teams, even if I had nothing to do with it!

York City was visited for their FA Cup match with Notts County and one final look on Paul Baker, then over to Gigg Lane to see the Foreign Legion play for Wigan at Bury in a scoreless draw, before returning to give my reports to John and watch the by now regular occurrence of a 2 - 0 defeat at home to Lincoln City.

Shortly after Swindon's Autoglass exit at home to Hereford United which saw the entire Swindon support stand and cheer former player Steve White returning to the club and scoring the only goal, Steve McMahon released a batch of players including defender Jamie Pitman, whose mother is the racing trainer Jenny. As soon as I told John he was on the phone to John Trollope at Swindon and every attempt possible was made to get Jamie to come down to the club. He decided that the team bottom of the Football League was not for him and went off to join the Swindon old boys at Hereford. This was to be an on going problem for other players as well, made worse with the Stevenage legal problems for plans and budgets to be put together for this season.

October 1995 will also be remembered by all at the County Ground with sadness as it marked the passing of Kevin Morris who had been the Physio at the club for many years. He had become worried about the prospect of him losing his job and committed suicide in his car which became filled with fumes from a pipe leading from the car's exhaust.

I met up with Paul Compton and John at Keynesham FC for Torquay Reserves 2 - 2 draw with Bath City and bumped into a few old faces including Gary Smart who had just joined Bath after a few years at Wokingham and Oxford United. The Gulls were now going through a purple patch and enjoyed the luxury of an away point at Northampton in a 1 - 1 draw, my first match at the new Sixfields Stadium having visited it many times in the past with my former contractor. Then to Walsall for the match of the season, an FA Cup 2nd Round Replay. Torquay were winning only to lose a late goal and miss a goal themselves with the last kick of the 90 minutes which finished 3 - 3. Extra time then arrived and we were left to count the cost of that missed opportunity in the 90th minute when Walsall went on the rampage and the game finished an exhausting 8 - 4 to Walsall.

An approach was made to Dean Sturridge at Derby County, but he was not for sale and did not want to join Torquay on a permanent basis, he knew his own potential and the club was not where he saw his future.

An Anglo Italian game at Luton and league matches at Swindon and Portsmouth passed and a trip to the Orient to watch some of my former colleagues from Rochdale lose 2 - 0, before the New Year was ushered in. I had custody of the kids so had a party with half the street present. After dropping the children back home I drove to Devon and the hangover was made worse by watching Mark Kinsella destroy Torquay. The worst bit was having Torquay kick off and find themselves 1 - 0 down within 19 seconds after Mark intercepted a sloppy back pass to Ashley Bayes and scored. Torquay to their credit fought back and were winning 2 - 1 with ten minutes to go when Colchester upped the pace and forced an equaliser, not content with a draw they scored the winner with the last kick of the game to go home 3 - 2 victors. It was not to be our season!

Paul Baker eventually agreed terms and signed towards the end of January to reinstall some hope in the supporters along with Aiden Newhouse on loan from Wimbledon who after missing two absolute sitters at Exeter City of all clubs, The fans were starting to worry about how they were going to get to Hednesford. This made the club's wage bill the highest in Torquay's history and to justify the expense the fans were needed to continue to turn up at matches to help make ends meet.

I was asked to keep my eyes open and report back any findings but the chances of the club signing any further players were now almost nil so after Christopher had decided to take the afternoon off school and come with me to see Swindon Reserves draw
0 - 0 with Southampton so I could watch former Alloa Midfielder Paul Sherrin play for the Saints I had the luxury of watching two matches in the Premiership, at Aston Villa v Tottenham Hotspur and West Ham v Manchester United, before being brought down to earth with matches at Oldham (v Barnsley) and Millwall (v Portsmouth).

Following a glorious one match unbeaten run hopes were raised then shock horror a second win both 2 - 1 firstly with Orient then Fulham, both at home And for the rest of the season the teams left the pitch to the sound of the theme to the "Great Escape" sounding in their

167

ears. It was to be extremely apt! Mike Bateson became a Stevenage Borough supporter as the only way the club would survive in the League would be if Stevenage won the Conference as their ground was not up to League Standard. As a safe guard for the club's own facilities standards The Popular Side underwent further development with the inclusion of an Indoor Bowls room for the local community and a stairway was created to the TV Gantry to improve on the existing ladder which had been around since the year dot!

I came down for Bath City's return fixture with the reserves, Paul was away so John, myself and Kevin Hodges stood by the dugout observing. I informed Kevin of Gary Smart being in good form but our youngsters did not heed the advice and Gary scored twice and set up the other two goals as Bath won 4 - 1. A frustrated spectator hurled abuse at me as he left also calling the side rubbish, but Mike had the last laugh by axing the reserve team and Paul at the end of the season.

Three Swindon matches and a trip to Merseyside to see Charlton lose 2 - 1 to Liverpool in the 5th Round of the FA Cup took some of the Devon pressure off and for a laugh I promised a friend and one of the Swindon Town Ladies team, Claire Tyson that I would go along and watch. I did and saw them win 12 - 0 against another ladies team Leighton Linslade, it was actually quite amusing to watch with the standard comparable with Sunday Pub Leagues but the girls tried hard and I was actually impressed by a couple of the players. It was a little disheartening to find out that one of the ladies who was reasonably attractive was a lesbian, but you can't have it all I suppose!

I returned to Wokingham Town to sponsor their match with Marlow. Steve Darlington was again scoring as Town won 2 - 0. After the match I started to get the feeling that the club directors were not to my satisfaction. I took some guests in and was approached whilst eating the buffet and the Chairman in front of my guests demanded to know what I was doing in the board room. After explaining I was the sponsor, I was told that the match did not have a sponsor. My reply was:

"Have you read the programme?",

to which a no was received. On checking the directors were more humble but I lost a lot of respect for them. This disappeared completely at the start of the following season! I used the opportunity of having a grovelling Chairman to my advantage and said that Roy Merryweather had been at the club for over 30 years without reward. If I were to organise a testimonial for him could the club provide the facilities free of charge. This was readily agreed so I went to work and contacted Dennis Smith. Maurice Evans then took over as he had known Roy for many years and agreed to send the Oxford first team along. Oxford did not have a match one weekend so Maurice went to Abingdon to see Wokingham play and mentioned the Testimonial to the same director who had agreed the match. The director denied all knowledge so Maurice contacted me. After a few phonecalls the match was back on again with Roy now feeling piggy in the middle as he had not officially been told the game was going ahead. The directors moaned about loss of revenue so we agreed that the club would keep all bar profits and Roy would keep the gate receipts and the profit from the raffle/ auction. Ross MacLaren provided a signed Swindon shirt, Dennis agreed to bring something signed by Oxford on the night and Eddie provided a signed Torquay shirt. Stevenage Borough contacted Maurice about a pre season friendly and only one date was free in the club's diary so he turned them down and set the date for the Wokingham Testimonial for Tuesday 30th July at Finchampstead Road. Ann Gale and I agreed to edit the programme and all the usual helpers were on hand free of charge. Even the match officials wanted to do it free out of respect for Roy. So everything was set and we awaited the start of the next season.

Meanwhile, the air of doom and gloom was descending on Torquay following bad performances at Wigan and a long injury list. Veteran Simon Garner was brought in as cover but with budgets now exceeded it was up to the youngsters to pull their weight. Long term supporter Helen Chamberlain was presenting Soccer Am on Sky Sports 2 and apart from getting a lot of stick from other fans phoning in to the Sunday morning show, the club were getting a lot of positive publicity. Helen was enjoying matches in the directors box sitting in the top far right hand seat and pre and post match sessions in the boardroom, before joining members of the 200 club in the players lounge for chats. She became very popular, being extremely attractive also helped as everyone swarmed round her at away matches to speak to her. I became jealous of not being able to attend every match with her, and I know of several supporters who turned out to see her and not the team on Saturday afternoons.

Swindon played at the Manor and Andy banned me from sitting anywhere near him for the game. I took along two Swindon supporters and sat about five rows behind him. As United won 3 - 0 no problems occurred in the ground and a lot of smiling faces were on show in the players lounge after the match. The club even went so far as to release the whole 90 minutes on a video through the club shop and Tee Shirts appeared depicting an Oxford logo as a raging Bull with the words Mad Ox BSE

(Beats Swindon Easily) a joke at the expense of the resident beef crisis and poking fun at Swindon. I saw the funny side of it and the shirts sold out within 90 minutes of them going on sale, unfortunately the Swindon Press went to Town on it and stirred up a heated debate which caused a lot of ill feeling in Swindon over it. The whole incident started as a joke but got out of hand with threats of the club being reported to the League for bringing the game into disrepute. I overheard a Torquay supporter talking about Grecian 2000 referring to Peter Fox's attempts to rid himself of grey hair instead of the club building a new ground before the turn of the century. No Exeter fan would be upset it is all light hearted terrace humour between rival clubs, only the press make an issue of matters and cause the resentment themselves by the manner in which they report news!

Mike came under fire from supporters for turning over the Popular side to the opposition for the visit of Plymouth Argyle. As the level of support was dropping and Plymouth were bringing a large support with them allocating them in one larger area was for the best interests of everyone. More fans could see the match so allowing extra income missing from the stay away fans plus putting the supporters together meant easier stewarding and improved safety for all concerned. However, some old moaners did not see it that way and accused Mike of making a fast buck and boycotted the match. These so called supporters were very short sighted and give the chairman no end of abuse which is quite frankly uncalled for. He had his own company which he made a success and sold it off, he put a lot of his own profit into the club and not retired to the Caribbean. The company got into trouble so he bought it back very cheaply made it a success again then sold it off. Again a lot of the profits going into the club. He paid for the redevelopment of the ground but the fans forget this and hurl abuse at him for the teams performances. He funded the mercenaries in the first place, if they let the fans down then it is the players fault not Mike's. If he had sold the club and walked away. Torquay United would not be in existence today. Perhaps after some careful consideration from the frustrated supporters they might decide to leave him alone and support the team as without support and no money coming in what is the point of playing. Mike's pockets of cash are not endless and why should he continue to finance a club were the fans turn there backs on him and the team? A situation no doubt felt at quite a lot of similar clubs nation-wide!

After being with Debbie on my birthday the previous year and Andy having made plans for hers, My 31st was spent at the Manor Ground watching a 0 - 0 draw with Wrexham, and a 3 - 2 win for Swindon over Brighton the following night. Then TV coverage actually did me a favour for a change and the Charlton v Luton match was chosen for coverage in the Carlton TV region on Good Friday so off I went and met Paul Clayton for my first visit to the new East Stand. The sight of alcohol being served in the bar behind the stand took me back a few years, but the facilities were truly impressive. No queues in the toilets either was a major boost and I was happy that I had decided to visit the new stand. The last time I was in it was when Roy King gave me a guided tour whilst it was under construction. I prefer that stand now and will always use it when visiting the Valley.

A 1 - 1 draw was slightly marred by fighting in the away stand, but it was good to be back. Swindon v Notts County and Wycombe Wanderers v Oxford United on Easter Monday brought a hectic holiday period to a close.

Going back to High Wycombe was one of those days when I wished the ground would open up and swallow me as a slight oversight by Andy caused me a lot of embarrassment! We repeated the previous years itinerary and met up in the local pub. My first comment was to walk up to former director Paul Lowe and ask where his wife Katherine was. A silence went round the pub. He had left her to go off with his secretary and as Andy hadn't told me was completely unaware and well and truly put my foot in it. Lisa quickly changed the subject and I was promptly led away and put in the picture. Paul turned round in the queue at the turnstiles to put his side of the story whilst the others were putting a bet on at the ground's bookmakers. They both still attend matches and sit a few rows apart in the Manor Club, but the best is in the players lounge after the match where they ignore each other and all Andy's friends take it in turns to move between the two to make conversation in between Les trying his luck at chatting her up everytime I attend matches at the ground.

I had still got 18 matches to go till the end of my season as the London 5 a sides had been cancelled and although I was present at all the remaining Swindon home matches and midweek Oxford matches fitted in eight senior non league matches in a bid to prepare for the coming season. Torquay had finished bottom of the league and Eddie had resigned. Stevenage had won the conference but were to take legal action against the League and Torquay for not allowing them to be promoted an anxious close season was to follow!

Above: Swindon's Ross MacLaren presenting me with Jan Aage Fjortoft's Norway Shirt

Right: Enjoying life at Torquay United

Chapter 16

Betrayal

The week leading up to the Wokingham v Oxford match were getting frustrating. The directors were still not confirming the match and avoiding me. John Aulsberry the Secretary had confirmed in writing with Oxford so the game was going ahead. I had further helped the club by providing some more supplies at cost to keep down the club's debt and as a result Roy was allowing my company to sponsor the game for free. My girlfriend at the time Beverley had a friend who had just moved to Wokingham to marry one of the Town's footballers so she came along also to meet up with Jasmin. Only trouble was that she split from her husband a few days before the match so Beverley watched the game as well. Roy had laid on a buffet as usual for us in the boardroom and went out of his way to try and calm me down. The directors had finally decided a few days before the match that the club needed the money more than Roy and put Roy in an awkward position of having to agree and used the game as a friendly only. Roy's son Kevin warned me the day preceding the match so I was able to keep my calm about the betrayal. I had been used by the directors of the club, who obviously had no intention of honouring Roy at all. Not only that the stab in the back had left me with egg on my face as far as Maurice Evans and Oxford United were concerned. They had used Maurice and the clubs who had generously donated items for the raffle. I gave the raffle items directly to Roy to avoid further profits going the way of the club. Maurice did as he had promised and Dennis Smith brought the entire first team down for the fixture which United won 3 - 1. Lisa, Roger, Les, Richard and Paul Lowe were in attendance, but Andy was missing having not felt very well during the day. After the match Dennis said hello to me but not much else as the players tucked into the buffet provided. I knew what he was thinking but to avoid an incident didn't raise the testimonial issue. The worst part of the whole evening was the entire bunch of Wokingham

Directors drank and ate in the same room as me and avoided me the whole time. It was probably for the best as if one of them had dared cross my path it would have sparked me off. I have not seen Maurice Evans since the week before the match and would love to know his feelings on this issue. My loyalties are now only with Roy Merryweather. As far as I'm concerned the club has lost my sponsorship and a lot of possible future friendlies with sides I have contacts with, so the directors short sightedness has blackened the image of the club and a short term gain will be met with long term debts. I at one stage considered highlighting this in the local press, but it would probably mean Roy suffering a backlash from those who can't be trusted so I avoided making a public issue over the event, but I am still very angry about it!

The pre season friendlies kicked off at Enfield with Arsenal's 1 0 victory then up to renew old acquaintances at Halifax Town and watch Rochdale who did not contain many familiar faces in the side that won 2 - 1. Glenn Hoddle kept his word through Ruud Guillet to provide the Chelsea first team for a memorial match for the late Swindon physio Kevin Morris and a near capacity crowd turned out to see the blues beat Swindon 2 - 0. Unlike Wokingham the directors kept their word and Kevin's widow and family received a bumper payout to help keep them in the years ahead.

Visits to Chesterfield, Bashley, Tiverton and Cheltenham followed as I had a look at some of the younger and cheaper talent that was around before heading for Clevedon Town of the Beazer Homes League.

Kevin Hodges had stepped up from YTS Officer at Torquay to the position of joint player coach. His joint colleague being Gary Nelson which gave me great delight. I drove to Clevedon to see Gary after Torquay's 1 - 0 friendly victory in which he scored the only goal after about 30 seconds but after the match saw Chris Carter and another friend approaching Gary so knowing those two would be chatting for hours left them to it. Kevin also had a turn out on pitch as he has retained his players registration.

Midweek I went to see my old friend Terry Brown now manager of Hayes Town in the Conference, He was a little upset by the game we watched as Brentford tore his side to shreds winning 7 - 0. Which led me nicely to the start of the season. Beverley had suggested that she had never been to Torquay and was fascinated by the club so having a weekend off from the children we had a lovely romantic weekend in Torbay staying at the Kistor Hotel and going on to Plainmoor for the first game of the season at home to Lincoln City. This is where I had my first surprise of the weekend. Chief Scout, John James had quit the team to defect to Plymouth Argyle and not told me. I was very unsure of my position, although Kevin later confirmed it was not in jeopardy.

The season kicked off on a high with Paul Baker and Rodney Jack combining well together up front and the inclusion of several new players. Rhys Wilmot had been persuaded to add his vast experience to the side having played in goal at Arsenal and Crystal Palace amongst others. Jon Gittens came over from Portsmouth, And Steve McCall joined from Plymouth as player coach with responsibilities for Youth Development. All this was to cost money so the admission prices were raised from £5 to £8 for adults to assist with the funding. This was not universally accepted by the fans who at £8 were still being treated to the cheapest admission prices in the League! Efforts were being made to prolong the club's stay in the league and to put it into context, when Alan Shearer transferred to Newcastle United for £15 million Mike went to print with a piece in the programme stating that it "Represented 45 years turnstile takings at current rates!"

Attracting some decent players became impossible over the summer because of the ongoing court case saga with Stevenage Borough. Players did not want to commit to a club that was playing in the GM Vauxhall Conference, by the time matters had been sorted out most of these players had been snapped up. I had suggested to Eddie prior to his departure that the club produce a record with the team singing the theme from Monty Python's Life of Brian. The "Always look on the bright side of life" song was quite apt and to release footage of the misses against Exeter on a video and finish up with a shot of Stevenage's ground. He thought it was a great idea and would appeal to a lot of fans, but decided against it because of how extreme Borough were taking the League's decision. Rules were rules and whilst I agree with Stevenage about the 31st December ground deadline they knew the rule before starting the season and had to abide by it. The time for changes had to be made before a ball was kicked so everyone was aware of it. What the club were doing was to attempt to push the League into changing their minds. They have done so with different views of the same rules before. A direct example was the relegation of Swindon Town three Divisions for irregularities after they had won promotion to the top flight, but a top Premiership club were found guilty of the same breach in the regulations and only fined. This caused a lot of aggravation and calls for compensation at the county ground. The League must stick to the rules and be consistent otherwise the inconsistencies will create more occasions where member clubs will go to court to challenge its authority.

The Lincoln game finished with a 2 - 1 victory to Torquay following a rare goal from Jon Gittens and a piece of ball control mastery from Rodney Jack and his resulting shot from outside the box in the last minute giving us the win we badly needed as most of the football world were watching on with interest to see what we would do back in a league higher than we should have been in.

The second shock of the weekend occurred on getting home when Beverley received a phone call from her previous boyfriend who was now back in the country. She made a few excuses and dumped me to return to him. That was the end of one more relationship consigned to the EX - FILES!

The next two months were spent commuting between Oxford United and Swindon Town for matches including taking Christopher to see Tottenham Reserves win 3 - 1 at Swindon in the Football Combination. I was keeping an eye on Dean Hooper who was in the Town Reserve side and in October released by Steve McMahon.

A brief revisit to Scotland brought recommendations of two strikers: Peter Dwyer at my old side Alloa who had just scored 5 goals

177

in 7 matches before going to Australia for a wedding which meant interest had to be cooled off on him and Scott Taylor at Montrose who had scored 6 goals in 5 consecutive matches. In an attempt to keep costs down I enrolled Peter Gibson and team manager Tom Hendrie at Alloa to keep me informed of any quality players that they see and allow me to pass the information onto Kevin and Gary. Another former colleague Malcom Drewitt had accepted a football coaching position in America and was prepared to assist and promised to send reports on any talent emerging over Stateside before the larger clubs get to hear about them. The network was expanding as Kevin and Gary were also using their contacts and a very cheap and efficient scouting network was starting to take shape.

I felt a bit of a fool on 19th October travelling over to the other side of Swindon to the Allied Dunbar Sports Club. I went to give Peter Distin and the Torquay Youth team some support and duly arrived in the club's run out top and tracksuit expecting to see them take on the Swindon Youth team in the South West Counties League. I was the only one to turn up! The changing rooms were open and the fixture one of three chalked up on the noticeboard, but no players or officials. The game had been called off early to stop a wasted trip by the boys but this decision had not been made public. I shall try again in the rearranged game in the new year!

Chans, or Rodney Jack to the rest of us had started to attract the interest of leading clubs and is a current St. Vincent international, flying back to the Grenadines regularly to take part in the country's World Cup qualifying matches in between matches for Torquay. Whilst a quiet lad at times he has a bit of a reputation around the club for being a ladies man and is very popular in the town. So it came as no real surprise when Kevin Keegan offered the club £300, 000 for him. Chans went up to have trials with Newcastle, but the deal is still in the melting pot as he signed direct for Torquay from the Caribbean and needs to play in a minimum of 75% of the first team matches to retain his work permit and Kevin can not guarantee him that. This then alerted other clubs to the skilful player.

By the time I had paid my monthly trip to the club and seen a 1 - 0 victory over Doncaster Rovers the team was flying high and things were looking rosy from the outside. However, cracks were starting to appear which was to lead to a bad run of results. Rodney was away on World Cup duty and Paul Baker had returned up north much to the disgust of the fans. A lot of anger was vented at Mike Bateson although there was little he could do about it. Bakes's wife Beverly and his children had remained up north when he joined from York City and with the birth of his third child Beverly was adamant that she was not going to move down south and this put a lot of pressure on Paul who in my view did the right thing and stood by his wife and asked to be transferred so he could spend more time with his family. If he had been made to stay the pressure would have got to him and he would have lost his form being not much use to the club. He is now still scoring at Scunthorpe United and settled. We are all pleased for him that he is happy, but some of the supporters were unaware of the facts and turned on Mike by cheering Paul's name on the terraces following the 2 - 0 defeat against Colchester, long after he had left the club.

Richard (Dickie) Hancox left the club to pursue a career in other directions and would continue to play but at a lower level with Taunton Town. This would have caused a slight family rift as having married Debbie Bateson his father in law was the chairman of the club. Another to leave was Paul Adcock as Kevin informed him that the club would not be renewing his contract.

The stayaway supporters who are normally the ones making the most negative noises were given an ultimatum by Mike Bateson to turn up and maintain attendance's of about 3, 000 or measures would be taken, the first being the pulling out of plans to complete the ground redevelopment by adding a new covered stand at the away end. If the supporters were not prepared to come along and pay a token fee each match then why should he spend more money on the club? Next step would be the reduction of the wage bill to preserve club finances.

179

I continued to keep watching out as with Gary now injured the fire power up front had almost been extinguished. Charlton Athletic had made a few changes, Steve Brown and Paul Sturgess felt their first team chances were limited and David Whyte could not be guaranteed a first team place so had all been placed on the transfer list. Accompanied by my further reports on the club's two teenage talents Kevin Lisbie and Kevin Nicholls all of whom were known to Gary, both he and Kevin travelled up to Welling on Wednesday 27th November to see Charlton's reserves take on Oxford's reserve side. Next on the scouting hit list was the former Alloa midfielder Paul Sherrin playing at Southampton and a few others which I am unable to mention here as alerting the club and player would only artificially increase his price and cause Kevin a headache!

Paul Sherrin was released by Graeme Souness at Southampton and several other clubs were watching him closely. I was given the exact facts in the Oxford United players lounge by some of the Southampton players after the 1 - 1 draw in the Coca Cola Cup. It was a little frustrating to report back to Kevin and find that Mike had put his foot down on the club as attendance's were falling as rapidly as the team were sliding down the league table and a decision was made to cut the wage bill. Initially by not replacing those players that were leaving. So I attended the evening match with Rochdale on 3rd December. Mike Morgan had not been to the club for a match in 12 years but enjoyed the business that Chester City gave him every year when they stayed at the Kistor Hotel prior to playing Torquay. Cedric Munslow gave me some information that led to Scarborough staying also prior to their game two weeks later, so I took him to the ground and he was pleasantly surprised at the excellent facilities available and just how many people he knew in the 200 club. Carlsberg Tetley who provide the alcohol to this hotels have an executive box and he now has access to it whenever he pleases. The business opportunities now available to him were quickly realised. This was just one incident of a local businessman not realising the potential of increasing his own business through contacts made by joining the club. If more came along it would make Cedric's job a lot easier in the Commercial Department and the increased revenue into the club would ensure that the wage bill was met and a continuity of quality players on the pitch.

Newcastle United were live on TV and added to the bad run of 5 straight losses all without scoring, shortly to be made 6 when Rochdale won 1 - 0 meant a poor turn out of 1, 086. To put that in perspective with gate receipts of £4, 000 having to last a club a fortnight which currently pays out between £8 - £10, 000 per week on wages it does not take much of a mathematician to calculate that steps need to be taken, and quickly.

Helen Chamberlain was as usual in the director's box being accompanied by her fellow Sky presenter Andy Gray, who enjoyed a pre match tour of the facilities. Kevin joined me in the players lounge after the match and he said:
"Thanks for your efforts and to keep up the good work".
Its nice to know from time to time that my efforts are appreciated! Both he and Cedric are by now used to my little eccentricities when I am at the ground, even if Cedric tends to think I'm slightly potty at times, my actions have always been in the best interests of the club.

Having sat in my seat directly in front of the Director's Box a familiar face appeared who recognised me. Trevor Senior, whom I had not seen face to face since my early days with Reading. He had retired from playing and was living in Dorchester and had come along with Paul, who was manager at Bridport Town in the Beazer Homes League. Knowing Bridport's President Barrie Williams very well Paul was easy to get on with. Trevor had been asked by Maurice Evans to scout for Oxford and have a look at Rodney Jack. He had also been looking at Paul Sherrin, so with the news that the club could not afford any further purchases in the immediate future I was more than able to assist my former colleague and Maurice by providing some background information on both Paul and Rodney. Having scouts watch Chans is becoming quite a regular occurrence and I doubt if he will still be a Torquay player at the end of the season. Gary is currently preparing a follow up to his previous book highlighting his first season in management so although we will probably end up cross referencing each other, he will have the last word on the subject with his latest autobiography.

Mike Bateson was raving before the match, but by the end and the so called fans were openly shouting abuse at him he was more relaxed having deadened the nerves in the boardroom. However, the losses need to be addressed and if the fans are not prepared to turn up then a major change could happen. Mike hinted that the club may have to follow the Scottish Lower Leagues and be forced to go part time within the Football League. He said:

"The fact is that the game has changed, and we've got to get to grips with it. Part-time football within the Third Division will be a reality for somebody this season or next. That club may be Torquay United!"

Christmas is traditionally the season for farce and 1996 was to be no different, only this time it was to be on and off the football pitch! The weather was extremely cold and icy with several games being called off for frozen pitches. Not so at Swindon who finished the year off in style with a skating spectacular against Grimsby Town. Hardly a move was possible without a player sliding. After a Grimsby player had been sent off and Graham Watson had scored a blinder from outside the box to give Swindon a 30 minute lead, the game was called off because of the state of the pitch. Being a former referee I totally agreed with the referee's actions, but as it was clear from kick off how dangerous the conditions were the game should never have been played. Because of his indecisiveness the referee left the pitch to the sound of jeers and boos from the crowd, who felt cheated and extremely cold. I felt sorry for the single coach load of Grimsby fans who had to face another long journey for the rearranged fixture later in the season.

That was the icing on the cake for me having wasted my time flying to Scotland to see my old colleague Ally Dick who had returned from playing in Australia and South Africa to Scotland to look for a full time club. Until he found one he was training with Alloa. I was unable to see him play in their game with Inverness Caledonian Thistle as it was called off for a frozen pitch. I took the first flight back to catch the Swindon game and the above paragraph says it all!

Things did not improve as a cold spell swept the country and most games fell victim to the weather well into the new year. I travelled to Vicarage Road to see the Watford v Oxford F A Cup 3rd Round tie. The game was postponed one minute from kick off because of the frozen pitch, and the fans were not too happy with the referee's decision. Fortunately for Andy and myself we were in The Henkel Executive box enjoying the excellent hospitality provided by both the club and the boxes owners. But being in the warm was little comfort for not seeing the cup tie. We returned the following Tuesday for the rearranged fixture and had just finished our meal in the box when with 20 minutes to go to kick off the floodlights failed. Here we go again was the general consensus, before an Oxford Supporter came to the rescue as an employee of an electricity company and during the hour's delay he re-routed the power to allow the game to go ahead. This did have its draw backs as no power was available to light the ladies toilets or serve hot drinks at the kiosks. Most of the Oxford fans then begged him to switch the lights back off again as Watford won easily 2 - 0.

Off the pitch trouble was brewing in the ground development side. In the wake of the Hillsborough tragedy all grounds were to have meet a new minimum requirement for safety by 1998. Torquay being one of the more fortunate ones to be in advanced stages of redevelopment. For other clubs to finance such a project was out of the question so grants were set up to help fund the modernisation of the stadiums. However, the week following Christmas a further body blow was dealt to the lower league clubs who after losing out in the Sky TV deal now found themselves suffering further following an announcement by the Football Trust that they had placed a stop on all future grants for ground development. The trust is funded by a reduction in Pools Betting Duty Tax which is then passed to the clubs via the trust to assist financing the work required by the Taylor Report.

The National Lottery is certainly doing its bit with regard to helping sport but now we can see the other side of the coin and we can clearly identify those areas which have been adversely affected by the change in the public's gambling habits then it is surely time for the government to get a grip and require that the shortfall is addressed for both the clubs and supporter's sakes!

Football, although a global sport it is a small world within the game and everyone ends up knowing each other and eventually bumping into each other like I did with Trevor Senior, or the influence that Maurice Evans has had on me over the years. Life goes on and a lot more will change before the end of the 1996 - 97 season. What will happen to me?

On the personal and business side of my life I have received so many kicks in the teeth that I have no teeth left to remove. I have recently suffered badly on the health side but all three have bottomed out and the turn is now upwards and I look forward to attempting to make a success of my life. I have both my lovely children by my side and an unbreakable bond with the best friend any person could ever ask for in Debbie. And some extremely close friends with Caryn and Mandy to name but two!

I have made several appearances on TV as a TV extra recently, so watch out for more appearances in the future! I did some photo modelling for an agency in early 1996 and found myself staring at my photo on German TV over Christmas as I was channel hopping. They had obviously purchased the photo from the agency and were using it to promote a 0190 chat line in Germany. It was for a gay line and used three photos of "real males" so I don't know whether to be happy or not about the way it was used. Still I took my money when I was paid for the photo shoot so I have to take the rough with the smooth in that game. Musically, I used to help out at a rock club in Wokingham and helped as a rode in the early eighties for Motley Crue and Shakatak when they came to town. Whilst working in Cobham I got to know the Moody Blues quite well as they lived in the area and opened their own record store - Threshold Records a few doors down from my shop. But I am too old for that sort of thing now, so I will restrict myself to listening to CD's only now. However, both Frances and her boyfriend Phil are trying to re educate me in music and take me out to see some of the local bands. Some like Hot Rocks are very good, but their is a lot of rubbish playing and some of the pubs are real dives. When we go I adopt a quiet approach and become similar to my mate Mel and become a people watcher. I find it fascinating to see the type of person that goes to these gigs and certain dross bands attract similar personalities. Whilst I am never the life and soul of the party I am fairly out going and very friendly so am very popular with my laid back attitude and approach to life. Some may feel awkward because of the nature of my friendliness, but that is me and I am not about to change my style just to please a few who may misjudge my motives. Most of the people who are wary of me are men as us guys are meant to be mean and keep themselves to themselves. Probably because of this attitude I find myself with lots of female friends and few male friends. I always appear to be the girls best friend, this is fine but can be a problem if I were to take the relationship a stage further as they don't want to risk losing my friendship, should anything go wrong with the relationship. It can be frustrating at times!

The Porsche Club of Great Britain have appointed me as Register Secretary for the 924 models which should keep me busy not only compiling a database on the PC for them, but organising several events for its members. My companies continue to trade and I am training individuals on basic computer literacy when I can get the contracts. I have assisted with several departments at Motorola and Ford over the past few months, where my sense of humour has nearly got me into trouble in the Customer Services Department on several occasions. Without thinking I answered a call from a Mr Hole who had a problem with his mobile phone. I was asked to contact his wife Mrs A. Hole with a solution and did not get a favourable reply when I told him

"I would look into it for him!"

Similarly when a Mr Hand from Barnsley asked for a phone for his wife and I offered him a second hand model!

This was followed by a call from a John Thomas looking into getting a Dictaphone as it came so close to the other call I had assumed it was my colleagues having a joke and treated it as such. Unfortunately the call was genuine and Mr Thomas was less than amused with some of the one liners that I had come out with. Things did however, get better after that and no further problems of note arose. Although I do blame the customers on occasions as I had to follow up a call to a Bill Monthly only to find out that the customer had a totally different name and had written in his invoicing instructions on the wrong line!

I am on the internet and being me can't resist a bit of good natured flirting. I correspond with several young ladies at the weekend including a Deb's, just to add further confusion having three already in my life!

As to the football side, well I will be at Charlton Athletic at the end of the season for a special presentation evening when I will be presented with Charlton player David Whyte's team shirt by him personally. At Torquay United, Kevin has assured me of my future as a scout for the club, but my playing days are well and truly over. I occasionally turn out to play 5 a side on a Thursday evening and that in itself is now my limit. I have put on weight since I stopped playing football so my new year's resolution is to lose it and the 5 a side will help and regular games of squash. I have games planned with my friend Liz Milburn at the Marriott Hotel for the new year and we both have agreed to make these dates as 1996 was full of constantly missed games because of work commitments. She works for Thomas Cook Travel and travels a lot. When she is in Swindon and based at Motorola in West Swindon, I am normally off elsewhere so our games never seem to get played for one reason or another.

February 1997 will see me gain an FA Coaching Certificate to add a further string to Kevin's bow should the cuts run even deeper at Plainmoor. I can draw comfort from the fact that as a former footballer I have faired better than a lot of my other colleagues. A good friend of mine, Eddie Murray being a typical example. He was very much a part of Swindon Town's Second Division Championship winning squad of last season. Steve McMahon released him and from comfortably earning £45,000 a year now finds himself having spent all his money, working in the warehouse at Ford Cellular in Swindon.

My journalism reached a high and I hope you have enjoyed reading about it in this book, and gaining a better understanding that the real life in football is not always on the pitch. A follow up may even appear one day, time will tell.

I have made many friends in the game and I hope those whose names have been omitted will forgive me for the oversight, and thank you for taking the time and interest to read this book!